Responsible Classroom Management

6-12

For all of our current and past students at UNC Charlotte.

J. Allen Queen | Bob Algozzine

6-12

Responsible
Classroom
Management

A Schoolwide Plan

CORWIN
A SAGE Company

For information:

Corwin
A SAGE Company
2455 Teller Road
Thousand Oaks,
    California 91320
www.corwin.com

SAGE Pvt. Ltd.
B 1/I 1 Mohan Cooperative
    Industrial Area
Mathura Road,
New Delhi 110 044
India

SAGE Ltd.
1 Oliver's Yard
55 City Road
London EC1Y 1SP
United Kingdom

SAGE Asia-Pacific Pte. Ltd.
33 Pekin Street #02-01
Far East Square
Singapore 048763

Printed in the United States of America

Library of Congress Cataloging-in-Publication Data

Queen, J. Allen.
Responsible classroom management, grades 6-12 : a schoolwide plan/J. Allen Queen, Bob Algozzine.
    p. cm.
Includes bibliographical references and index.
ISBN 978-1-4129-7413-4 (pbk.)
    1. Classroom management. 2. Behavior modification. I. Algozzine, Robert. II. Title.

LB3013.Q45 2010
373.1102′4—dc22   2010009469

This book is printed on acid-free paper.

10   11   12   13   14   10   9   8   7   6   5   4   3   2   1

Acquisitions Editor:	Debra Stollenwerk
Associate Editor:	Desirée A. Bartlett
Editorial Assistant:	Kimberly Greenberg
Production Editor:	Veronica Stapleton
Copy Editor:	Gretchen Treadwell
Typesetter:	C&M Digitals (P) Ltd.
Proofreader:	Charlotte Waisner
Indexer:	Kathleen Paparchontis
Cover Designer:	Rose Storey

Contents

Additional materials and resources related to
Responsible Classroom Management, Grades 6–12:
A Schoolwide Plan can be found at www.rcmplan.com

List of Tools

(Located in Resource B)

Acknowledgments

W e would like to personally thank the many teachers, principals, and graduate students who have used responsible classroom management (RCM) at different levels and researched the effectiveness of the model in the public schools. Of greater importance is our gratitude to the students who found success in the classroom through use of the many tools found in The RCMPlan™.

Special thanks go to the best editor in the publishing business, Debra Stollenwerk. Her guidance and direction provided us with the motivation to update the models and to prepare them in a more beneficial format for educators and students. Thank you, Deb. Also, thanks go to Julie for keeping us on schedule and for her personal care about our work. Last, but not least, thanks to Beth Blackwelder and Lee Mallen for their contributions on the original models that we have continued to build upon over the past fifteen years.

PUBLISHER'S ACKNOWLEDGMENTS

Corwin gratefully acknowledges the contributions of the following reviewers:

Inez Liftig

Grade 8 Science Teacher

Fairfield Woods Middle School

Fairfield, Connecticut

About the Authors

J. Allen Queen is a professor of educational leadership and former chair of the Department of Educational Leadership at the University of North Carolina, Charlotte. As a former classroom teacher, principal, college administrator, and university instructor, he has consulted in almost five hundred schools and districts, in forty-eight states and five foreign countries. He covers all areas of effective school discipline and responsible classroom management, and in addition, his work includes school violence and safe schools, successful student transitions, and drop-out prevention. He has written over fifty books and one hundred articles, including books for children on karate, in which he holds the rank of fifth degree black belt. He attributes his own sense of responsibility, civility, and respect, along with gains in self-confidence, to this martial art and popular sport. He has appeared on numerous radio and television programs, including *ABC World News*, where he was invited to discuss the problems that negative student transitions and ineffective classroom-management procedures have on school attendance and drop-out rates.

Bob Algozzine is a professor in the Department of Educational Leadership at the University of North Carolina, Charlotte, and project codirector of the U.S. Department of Education-Supported Behavior and Reading Improvement Center. With twenty-five years of research experience and extensive, firsthand knowledge of teaching students classified as seriously emotionally disturbed, he is a uniquely qualified staff developer, conference speaker, and teacher of behavior management and effective teaching. He is active in special education practice as a partner and collaborator with professionals in the Charlotte-Mecklenburg schools in North Carolina and as an editor of several journals focused on special education. He has written more than 250 manuscripts on special education topics, including many books and textbooks on how to manage emotional- and social-behavior problems.

Introduction

Be more ready than you think you will have to be.

—Robert Algozzine,
from *Teacher's Little Book of Wisdom*

As a middle or high school principal, could you use a school-wide discipline plan that lowers office referrals by 75 percent, decreases student suspensions more than 50 percent, and increases responsible student behavior that can be sustained at every grade level? Referred to as RCM or The RCMPlan™, responsible classroom management is a twofold program: (1) it teaches students to learn and internalize personal responsibility for their own behavior and (2) it serves as a well-tested, classroom-management plan for a schoolwide discipline model. For teachers, the book offers complete instructional plan for teaching responsibility and classroom management. For principals, the book offers a schoolwide discipline program that returns the control of non-violent behavioral problems back to the classroom teachers for resolution as part of the learning process. The RCMPlan™ allows the principal to refocus on instructional leadership and prevents an onslaught of the inappropriate-behavior situations that should be handled in the classroom. In addition, the book, along with an author-designed and monitored Web site, prepares the principal and selected training-team members to lead the faculty and staff in developing The RCMPlan™.

1

RATIONALE FOR THE RCMPLAN™

Student and/or classroom behavior encompasses the "biggest problem" facing our schools, as revealed in every one of the forty-one Phi Delta Kappa/Gallup public attitude polls (Bushaw & McNee, 2009, p. 10). Over the years, items such as discipline, lack of funding, drugs, and fighting/violence/gangs have topped the list. School administrators face daily and continuous challenges in efforts to establish and maintain safe and orderly classroom environments—where teachers can teach and students can learn.

One group or individual is not responsible for preventing and reducing behavior problems. Administrators need assistance identifying, implementing, and supporting effective interventions. Teachers need help teaching responsible and acceptable behavior along with academics. Students need to be taught appropriate social, behavioral, and academic norms, and then supervised in learning and demonstrating these norms. Parents need assistance participating as partners in making schools safer, more positive places to send their children. Preventing and reducing behavior problems, then, requires a schoolwide plan.

The RCMPlan™ provides a school-based model to work with all students. It is truly an individualized classroom-management plan, with two major goals: (1) to teach students to be responsible for their actions, and (2) to allow teachers and staff to use schoolwide discipline and a classroom-management plan that holds students responsible for all of their actions and behaviors. The RCMPlan™ also addresses the greater problem of student entitlement.

Students today often enter high school with a sense of entitlement that continues into college and adulthood. To explore this phenomenon, we conducted sessions with various groups of high school teachers, college professors, and employers. This "expected sense of entitlements," as one major CEO stated during a highly spirited focus group, manifests in actions once graduates enter the work force, with expectations for taking long breaks; leaving work early or arriving late; receiving special considerations for tasks; and wanting rewards, recognition, and praise for almost every job or task completed. College professors have shared similar feelings about students, especially among freshmen.

Customarily, teachers use bribes and rewards in the classroom to get students to behave appropriately and to complete assignments. The practice of bribery became prevalent in the 1970s when many parents were forced to develop a less demanding approach with their children as they experienced greater stress from working two jobs, returning to college, and other economic factors—all resulting in less time with their children. Either from guilt or excessive stress, parents found it easier to do previously child-oriented chores themselves, or to bribe children to complete tasks and even homework. Parents used this "reward-addicting" practice with children of all ages through high school.

In addition, we all have heard of "helicopter parents" hovering or intervening on their child's behalf at the college level. As former college administrators, it was not unusual for parents to confront us over a student's grade or a complaint about a specific professor. Teachers compound the bribery and reward problem by mastering this approach in preschool through high school. Today, these reward-addicted, entitled high school graduates now suffer from withdrawal after being bribed for years and often rewarded for substandard results. It is likely that many of these young employees or college students never fully learned to be responsible for their actions, or to act responsibly without an external source of validation.

RESPONSIBLE STUDENTS

Responsible students act with intended purpose based upon their own internal locus of control. Responsible students behave and act appropriately and complete academic assignments because it is expected in our culture. Responsible students have learned to treat teachers and other students with civility and respect. Many of these responsible students come to school from homes where bribes, treats, and rewards are *not* used as the major method of control. Some students learn responsible behavior by playing sports or participating in extracurricular activities. In a few situations, students are fortunate enough to have a strong teacher who works directly with students and willing parents to start reversing inappropriate habits, and teaching appropriate and responsible behavior.

Responsibility and civility cannot be ingrained until learned, practiced, and sustained. RCM provides the environment for students to learn and practice responsibility, while offering teachers and staff members tools for schoolwide use. These tools ensure sustainability and internalization of the newly learned behaviors. These are the goals of The RCMPlan™.

The belief that every student moves through several common developmental stages underlies RCM. These stages determine, to a high degree, the behaviors, attitudes, cognitive capabilities, and physical characteristics that a student will exhibit at any particular time. To assure that students prosper and develop into healthy and well-balanced adults, every student needs unconditional love, security, and the certainty of belonging.

The ability to discover workable solutions to all types of problems—academic, social, emotional, and personal—is fundamental to student success. RCM supports this learning and problem-solving ability, and in particular, focuses on social and academic contexts that mandate responsible and civil manners.

RCM assumes that most students, even the termed "problem students," can be taught to behave responsibly in school—operating within an internalized set of values and beliefs. Responsible students have learned to self-correct inappropriate behavior by using an internal locus of control. These students learned from the consequences of their behavior, and subsequently adjusted to expected behaviors and school and classroom standards.

BASIC RESEARCH SUPPORTING RCM

In our research on RCM, close analysis of almost any classroom reveals that approximately 88 percent of students never require major disciplinary actions. Although a teacher might have to restate expectations, most students generally behave appropriately. However, within the same classroom, approximately 12 percent of the students require varying degrees of the teacher's attention. Most of these students, three out of four of the 12 percent, are attention seekers or extremely active, and therefore require some corrective measures. The remaining students, or about 3 percent of the school population, exhibit anger, aggression, and mistrust in their behavior and attitudes. Their noncompliant behavior can be highly disruptive and usually requires special treatment to make the classroom an appropriate learning environment. As every teacher knows, the undesirable behavior of a single student can rapidly ripple through a class with devastating effects. The RCMPlan™ offers support for teachers in avoiding this situation and provides the tools to handle the most difficult student in the classroom.

Implementation of The RCMPlan™

Within the RCM classroom, students learn responsibility and are then expected to practice it. The RCMPlan™ defines a classroom-management system intended to teach students acceptable standards and guidelines with specific expected behaviors based upon their developmental levels. RCM allows teachers to monitor and guide students in nurturing, but accountable, ways. It also provides teachers with the independence to develop productive and stimulating classroom strategies that assist students in controlling their personal behavior. With The RCMPlan™, students willingly take an active role in developing and implementing classroom-learning experiences. As students take responsibility and develop accountability for their learning and self-discipline, they prepare for their future as mature and actively engaged adults.

ORGANIZATION OF THE BOOK

Principals and teachers begin their mastery of RCM after reading Chapter 1. Educators learn the three major principles used in The RCMPlan™ and how the discipline review committee (DRC) assists the principal and administrative team in preparing the faculty for personalizing the RCM model for their school. In Chapter 2, teachers learn more about the correlates from the researched schools and how to set up the instructional environment for teaching responsibility. Standards, guidelines, and expected behaviors are presented and discussed in detail in Chapter 3, with outcomes for schoolwide and classroom use. Chapter 4 supports these standards, guidelines, and behaviors with an array of RCM tools to maximize success of the program. Resource A and B offer guides for the principal and all teachers who will assist in the training for faculty and staff as they learn the basic principles and tools, and finalize the plan for the school.

LEADERSHIP AND DIRECTION FOR IMPLEMENTATION OF THE RCMPLAN™

The RCMPlan™ has been used with great success schoolwide at the elementary, middle, and high school levels. We have found that the direct success of The RCMPlan™ directly relates to the leadership provided by the principal in developing, implementing, monitoring, and evaluating this new model within the entire school building.

THE PRINCIPAL'S GUIDE

We provide the necessary steps and procedures for the principal to follow in preparing the faculty and staff for implementation of The RCMPlan.™ In table format, the guide is easy for the principal and other trainers to follow while leading faculty's staff-development activities for learning and using the model.

1. Steps and time factors

2. Staff-development activities

3. The RCMPlan™ book guide

4. The RCMPlan™ Toolbox

5. The RCMPlan™ Web site

THE RCMPLAN™ TOOLBOX

The RCMPlan™ Toolbox, in Resource B, works in conjunction with The RCMPlan™ Web site. Both contain activities and training guides, media sources, sample models, templates, and forms for implementing and sustaining The RCMPlan™.

These tools can be used as is, modified, or expanded in a school's design to assist in any training or communication surrounding The RCMPlan ™ Toolbox.

Principals and teachers can visit The RCMPlan™ Web site, www.rcmplan.com, without an ID login or password. In addition to supplemental training materials available for download, additional features on the Web site include a space for teachers to share ideas, locations and times for RCM seminars, and information on RCM master-training certification.

Our hope is for everyone implementing this program to make it their own with the greatest success possible. When implemented correctly, RCM provides a life-changing experience for students, teachers, and principals. As one middle school principal from Wisconsin professed—holding back tears—at the last seminar of a year-long pilot study, RCM not only saved his career, but also his life. The stress from losing control of a school, and knowing the low probability of ever regaining control, has cost many principals their positions and perhaps their health. We can't promise improved health, but if implemented as designed, remaining firm in the RCM concept, major decreases in office referrals and school suspensions will occur. Faculty and staff will also witness more responsible behavior in students and a general improvement in the school climate, resulting in a better team overall.

CHAPTER ONE

Understanding The RCMPlan™

Teach the three Rs: Respect for yourself, Responsibility for your actions, and Remembering the rights of others.

—Robert Algozzine,
from *Teacher's Little Book of Wisdom*

A HIGH SCHOOL CLASSROOM SCENE

To Rosemary Lopez, the new social studies teacher at Washington High, the early morning hall was alive with the usual noises: lockers slamming, friends yelling one more reminder as they charged in opposite directions, and too many feet dragging on the tiled floor. Next to Ms. Lopez's classroom, Lisa and Jon were right behind the door, whispering very seriously and holding each other as they did yesterday and the days before that. Clearly, school was not their primary concern, and Ms. Lopez's greeting only heightened their whispering. The indifference to education here was palpable.

Placing her coffee on her desk, Ms. Lopez was pleased to see that almost everybody was at their assigned desks—except, of course, Lisa and Jon, still holding, and Yoko and Robert, who were arguing in the back of the room. With the bell, Ms. Lopez expected full attention from the class,

(Continued)

9

(Continued)

and asked Thomas, sitting next to the door, to request Lisa and Jon's presence. Thomas, out of his seat before she even asked, attended to this regular early morning assignment. Yoko and Robert increased the volume of their exchange until Ms. Lopez could no longer restrain herself. She spoke to them as sternly as possible without showing her temper, yet was aware that her pitch was too high for effective intimidation; but somehow, she had to gain control. As the class watched nervously, she sarcastically asked Lisa and Jon if their marriage was faltering. The stratagem seemed to distract them. Yoko laughed, while Jon took offense and answered with a wisecrack about Ms. Lopez's ethnic group. His male friends hooted in approval . . . again, business as usual.

Ignoring the bait, Ms. Lopez asked the class to take out the individual assignments they had been working on for the last week. She could only hope that she had gotten on the right side of the contest by scoring a slight victory, temporary as it would be.

Damon waved his hand at Ms. Lopez and asked to present his materials first. Ms. Lopez looked around at the other hands, noting the expressions of those who did not volunteer as withdrawn and indifferent. She decided to ignore them; she could not afford to waste what little productive time she had to extract what they probably did not know anyway.

So, she quickly agreed to Damon's insistence, trying to move rapidly into the lesson without further distraction. Nevertheless, Robert asked, tauntingly, why he never got a chance to go first. Ms. Lopez saw her chance to embarrass Robert and asked Damon to allow Robert to demonstrate his knowledge. Robert said that he and Yoko had done the work together. Ms. Lopez replied that she was not interested in group work. She wanted to know what he was capable of—what he had done. Robert responded with sarcasm; this time directed at Damon. Kabir, Damon's friend, stared hard at Robert. Ms. Lopez felt her control become increasingly precarious.

Pushing hard ahead, Ms. Lopez proffered a short introduction, describing how she expected the class to carry on the discussion. The "squawk box" interrupted the effort with innocuous announcements. Ms. Lopez started over, clearly frustrated by the further delay. The class took precious minutes to refocus. Ms. Lopez then asked Damon to read his paper on the assigned issue of world population. She hoped the material would engage the class in something she considered important and immediate. She knew she was taking a chance, but the topic was in the news and certainly entwined in the study of world cultures. Within a few minutes, she realized she was right and wrong. The class was listening to Damon, but the class was also getting agitated as he confronted their preconceptions. They increasingly attacked his position and virtually everything he was saying.

Ms. Lopez recognized she needed to keep a tight lid on the discussion—quite opposite to what she had hoped. These discussions were laced with threads of racial, ethnic, and class conflict. She knew the backgrounds of her students; and, for many, she could guess their social and economic status. But as she looked at her class more closely, she realized that she did not really know them; she had not shared their experiences. She did not understand the extraordinary diversity of background, ability, and interest that confronted her. What could she do with this situation to make it work? Did she have the training? Did she have the skill? Could she succeed? What could she do to reclaim classroom management and teach effectively?

THE RCMPLAN™

The classroom scene illustrates a few moments of the complex dynamics and inherent potential for conflict in middle or secondary school classrooms in the United States today. Undoubtedly, this image is disquieting, but real. Compared to a decade ago, societal and personal conditions are more complex, harder to grasp, and more difficult to control. The nation's public schools absorb the pace and degree of these changes, and the individual classroom teacher stands at the core of the expected change process. The teacher likely depicts the perfect panacea capable of clearly manifesting the stability needed for behavioral and academic changes in our students. It is in this context that we introduce The Responsible Classroom Management Plan (The RCMPlan™).

The RCMPlan™ is a schoolwide, behavior-correcting plan that enhances a school's capacity to safely and effectively educate all students. The RCMPlan™ applies evidence-based support systems to maximize opportunities for teaching academics and prosocial behaviors. The following characteristics are embedded in the plan (Horner, Sugai, Todd, & Lewis-Palmer, 2005; Sugai, 2000; Sugai & Horner, 2002; Sugai, Sprague, Horner, & Walker, 2000):

- A team-based approach to identify, implement, and evaluate best practices, including administrators, teachers, school psychologists, other support personnel, and parents.
- Support for improvement efforts with budget, personnel, and resource allocations.
- Use of research-validated practices.
- Proactive behavioral instruction, teaching and modeling appropriate social behavior, with plenty of positive feedback.
- Opportunities for students to practice the expected behavior, aiming for fluency.
- A continuum of behavioral support to increase the intensity of the intervention as the intensity of the problem increases.
- Data-based systems and schoolwide, behavioral goals to guide decisions and keep staff informed on current guidelines along with what is and is not working.

Promoting good citizenship by developing responsible students who can live productively in a democratic and multicultural society is a key goal of responsible classroom management (RCM). This involves acting responsibly and practicing socially acceptable behavior. Responsible students also self-correct inappropriate behavior after they experience natural consequences for any inappropriate acts. William Glasser, in his book *Reality Therapy* (1990), defines responsibility as follows:

> . . . the ability to fulfill one's needs, and to do so in a way that does not deprive others of the ability to fulfill their needs. . . . A responsible person also does that which gives him a feeling of self-worth and a feeling that he is worthwhile to others. (p. xi)

Glasser believes students have certain needs that must be met by either the home or the school. When students behave inappropriately, it is because (according to Glasser) their basic needs are not being met. If the home does not satisfy those needs, then the school must try to meet them. Accordingly, the school and teachers must assist students in being successful in what they undertake—in their effort to learn, and in their pursuit of self-worth. It follows that if a student misbehaves in school, then teachers must somehow help the student meet unmet needs. If a student cannot adjust and behave more productively, then teachers must find ways to alter their own behavior, or the structure and contents of the classroom, to assist the student.

Taking a similar position to Glasser, RCM posits that teachers should not try to alter a student's world and allow the student to avoid the consequences of misbehavior. Changing the school environment is not the same as altering rules and expectations so that a student can avoid injury to self-worth. Rather, teachers should help students make value judgments about what causes a problem. When students judge their misbehavior and commit themselves to change, they will learn responsibility. Once a student commits to change, a teacher can accept no excuse from the student for not maintaining the commitment.

The RCMPlan™ ensures that a student is not permitted to escape responsibility for misbehavior. This does not mean that a teacher should punish or praise a student for a certain act, since this disconnects the student from directly accepting responsibility for the behavior. While punishment permits the student to focus on the punishment and the consequent feelings of revenge, praise motivates the student to seek similar commendation for any and all activity. Both practices thereby delay self-motivation. As an alternative, teachers must use logical consequences for the student to correct the misbehavior and develop responsibility.

BECOMING A SUCCESSFUL RCM TEACHER

To be successful, RCM teachers must analyze their own behavior to determine where they might inject unfavorable behaviors and attitudes into the classroom. Tendencies toward authoritarian or permissive control, prejudice, ignorance of the correct methodology, indecisiveness, or uncertainty about the goals of RCM will each undermine the RCM classroom and school.

According to the RCM perspective, external rewards in the form of reinforcement, or even casual praise, delay development of the responsible student. In a dynamic, creative, and uncontrived classroom, a teacher depends on the excitement from tapping a student's inherent need to know, learn, and very importantly, belong. RCM teachers derive a significant portion of stable behavior from excellence in instructional preparation and execution. Successful RCM teachers, then, carefully entwine **standards** and **guidelines** into the instructional process alongside **expected behaviors** supported by **natural and logical consequences**.

The Three Major RCM Principles

While The RCMPlan™ integrates many educational beliefs, three major principles maximize student success. These are listed and briefly addressed here, with much greater detail offered in later chapters about how these principles work in harmony to achieve all the desired behaviors discussed to this point.

The basic-program principles of The RCMPlan™ include:

1. Responsibility is taught and incorporated instructionally within a warm and inviting classroom.

The RCM approach to classroom management develops responsible students who can live productively in a democratic and multicultural society. Within the RCM classroom, responsibility is taught and then expected. Teachers, and the school organization, should implement democratic principles in their teaching and leadership roles. Human equality, dignity, self-worth, participation in decision making at all levels, and acceptance of the consequences of behavior should all be concepts integrated into the curriculum and consistently taught.

The school and classroom environment, and the concomitant instructional effort, embody the RCM approach. In a safe and inviting environment, a student feels secure and protected, and is then prepared to learn. The more positive the experience of the classroom, the greater the opportunity the teacher has to guide the students toward responsible behavior. Organization of space and time, format and presentation of instructional materials, the demeanor of the teachers, and the amount and kind of preparation are all critically important to success in an environmentally sound school and classroom. The RCM approach requires a teacher to clearly state the objectives of all planned classroom activity. This outcome-based approach to instruction necessitates the teacher's careful preparation and constant evaluation of student behavior. Precise and sensitive instructional guidance builds the foundation for responsible student behavior.

2. Standards, guidelines, and expected behaviors replace rigid school and classroom rules.

The RCMPlan™ does not use rules. Instead, the teacher uses standards, guidelines, and expected behaviors. Standards define the general direction of the desired behavior. Guidelines provide specific directions to successfully meet those standards, and expected behaviors represent grade level and developmentally appropriate actions to follow. In the RCM classroom, teachers act swiftly, consistently, and unemotionally to instill desirable behavior. As students learn to internalize responsible behavior, their self-esteem matures, and they increasingly gain internalized control over their own behavior.

3. Consequences teach students to self-correct inappropriate behaviors and assume responsibility for their actions.

Logical consequences link a student's inappropriate action to violated expected behavior, breaking the guideline and thus the standard. A logical consequence is not punishment. Instead, more realistic consequences result from not doing what is expected. For example, one guideline states, "The student is to come to school prepared to learn." In discussing this expectation, the teacher gives a directive for students to complete homework on a daily basis. Every student is expected to do the homework, with no exceptions. If a student comes in without his homework, he is not penalized with a low grade. Instead, he may be asked when he would like to complete the assignment—at break, during lunch, or after school. Those may be his only choices or there may be others. Specifically, the teacher may assign another consequence if she believes the initial one would not change the inappropriate behavior with this particular student. What happens if he doesn't have his homework in the future? One possibility is to simply repeat the consequence. Repeating a consequence can work well and proves that as teacher, she is serious. If the repeated consequence does not work, the teacher must move to something different with this student.

Individual Treatment

Within the RCM classroom, students are considered individuals who must be treated fairly and equally, but not necessarily the same. No parent disciplines two or three students in the same manner. For one student, time in her room is punishment and to another student, it is as a reward. Discipline, then, has to be personalized. Teachers achieve this with RCM and receive far less parental complaints than with other programs.

RCM fosters and acknowledges student performance and personal responsibility, and does not use bribery and predetermined rewards. Too often, teachers attempt to motivate students to learn and behave acceptably in the classroom with external rewards. This process is time-consuming, and often results in students who rely solely on extrinsic rewards to accomplish what should be intrinsically important to them. In contradistinction to this scheme, the RCM approach to classroom management uses high expectations and reasonable guidelines and standards to develop intrinsic motivation.

Students practice internal-behavior control rather than have their behavior controlled externally. Strict rules for obedience insulate students from personal responsibility—a result contrary to RCM purpose. When a student is taught to act autonomously, according to agreed-upon standards, the student acts responsibly. Responsible behavior does not require enforcement, and will likely be repeated without the application of external inducements. Much of the problem in our nation today with college graduates entering the workforce and demanding personal entitlements, we believe, stems from continuous bribes and rewards for completing assignments and/or simply behaving as expected.

A MODEL FOR IMPROVING INSTRUCTION AND BEHAVIOR

The thinking of humanist psychologists Abraham Maslow and Mortimer Adler, and cognitive developmentalists such as Erik Erikson, Richard Havinghurst, Lawrence Kolberg, and Jean Piaget, underlies The RCMPlan™. Based on this foundation, RCM shares some of the integrated ideas with the programs of Dreikurs, Nelson, and Glasser, but in a more practical and individualized manner.

RCM is based on the notion that every student moves through several common developmental stages. These stages determine, to a high degree, the behaviors, attitudes, cognitive capabilities, and physical characteristics that a student exhibits at any particular time. These proclivities, in combination with interactions with parents, siblings, peers, and teachers, greatly influence the pattern of behavior that a student adopts. To assure that students grow and prosper, and develop into healthy and well-balanced adults, every student needs unconditional love, security, and the certainty of belonging.

The ability to find workable solutions to life's problems is fundamental to a student's well-being. Within a hierarchy of learned behavior, the RCM model helps develop a capacity to solve problems. Students must be taught to examine and solve the many social and academic problems they will encounter during their growth. Accordingly, they must be given the opportunity to creatively and independently explore the world, define and achieve goals, and feel success upon which they will build self-assuredness, self-esteem, and ultimately, a strong self-concept.

RCM assumes that competent and responsible adults can teach most students, even so-called "problem" students and regardless of a student's socioeconomic or family history, to behave responsibly in the classroom, in school, and in the community at large. Behaving responsibly, according to RCM, means, in part, acting in accordance with an internalized set of values and beliefs, and with acceptance of the consequences of an act, whether positive or negative. On a continuum conveying degrees of responsible behavior, more responsible students self-correct behavior, use an internal locus of control, accept the consequences of their behavior, and follow guidelines to a greater degree than students who are less responsible. But regardless of where students fall on the continuum, most students can learn to behave responsibly. The real challenge lies in dealing with those few students—less than 5 percent of most classrooms—who exhibit anger, aggression, and mistrust in their behavior and attitudes. Their noncompliant behavior can be highly disruptive, and require exceptional treatment to make the classroom a viable operation. The RCM program addresses the needs of many of these students with the **intensive care unit** (a therapeutic removal from class, isolation, and counseling) and the team-led **discipline review committee**, both to be discussed later in this chapter. These tools use direct parent contact and establish two levels of contracts, **behavioral improvement agreements**, to include behaviors not responding to the previous plans. These tools function with appropriate consequences ranging from isolation, suspension, expulsion, and even entry into the juvenile justice system.

The Functions of the Discipline Review Committee

Classroom teachers use the intensive care unit (ICU) as a major consequence for significant disruptive classroom behavior, or intentional disrespect to a teacher or school employee. Students are removed from the setting where the offense has occurred and admitted to ICU. No work is permitted and the student must sit quietly and reflect upon the undesirable behavior. After the first visit to the ICU, the teacher meets with the student to establish procedures for avoiding a return to the ICU. Most students never return for a second visit. The discipline review committee (DRC), including parents and school administrators, monitors any rare second or third visits. No student is sent for a fourth time to ICU. Instead, a more severe consequence occurs. Usually by this time, the school is dealing with the top ten or so offenders in the entire school.

The DRC members, appointed by the principal or elected by the faculty, supervise all stages of The RCMPlan™. The DRC approves the overall school standard and guidelines, as recommended by the faculty and staff, and the chair serves as the major contact between teachers, students, and parents required to attend an ICU meeting. For each set of guidelines—such as behavior in the hall, parking lot, cafeteria, and other locations—a *specific* consequence correlates with the violation, including procedures for staff to follow. Prior to implementation or modification, the DRC must present the school's plan to the administration, faculty, and staff.

In the next step, individual teachers at the various grade levels and in special areas establish (or use the three we suggest) classroom guidelines (based upon school standards) and a pool of logical consequences for the classroom. After the first year, the faculty might seek student input as appropriate for revisions. This input allows students to be more involved in decision making and models participatory citizenship. Once the classroom plans are added to the school plan, the administration and staff establish an intensive care unit, prepare space, and develop a supervisory schedule. Two personnel are recommended to supervise the ICU at all times. The role of the DRC will be discussed in more detail in Chapter 4.

The ability to find workable solutions to life's problems is fundamental to a student's well-being. Within a hierarchy of learned behavior, the RCM model supports this capacity to solve problems. Students must learn to examine and solve the many social and academic problems that they will encounter during their growth. Accordingly, they must have the opportunity to creatively and independently explore the world, define and achieve goals, and experience success. Upon this, they will build self-assuredness, self-esteem, and, ultimately, a strong self-concept.

AN INVITATION TO CHANGE: THE RCMPLAN™ INVENTORY

Before beginning the RCM approach to schoolwide classroom management, reflecting on beliefs about students, teaching, and learning will help clarify one's professional knowledge and attitudes about the underlying principles of RCM. The RCMPlan™ inventory assists in this process, and requires a simple response from "agree" to "disagree," with "uncertain" gauging an uncommitted response.

Once the inventory is complete, compare your results to the "ideal responses" we suggest. Strong general agreement on the items suggests an understanding and compliance with the fundamental principles and practices of RCM. A strong general disagreement signals either misunderstanding or rejection of RCM principles. Uncertain responses indicate a lack of clarity surrounding RCM, the meaning of a particular statement, or one's own values and practices. This is a crucial step because potential users must understand and agree with the driving principles of RCM for it to be successfully implemented. By examining responses, you can identify areas of concern and further explore the underpinnings of RCM before proceeding.

If you don't feel prepared to take the inventory at this time, revisit it after you finish other chapters or the entire book. Use the inventory individually or use it with the entire faculty for training, keeping in mind that it is not just an inventory—it is a teaching tool.

The RCMPlan™ Inventory

	Rating		
Item	*Agree*	*Uncertain*	*Disagree*
1. Students and adults move through common developmental stages that affect their behavior.			
2. Teachers should ignore student misbehaviors and smile or wink when acceptable behavior is observed.			
3. Students should be taught problem-solving methods.			
4. Self-assuredness, self-esteem, and a strong self-concept are fundamental to success in school.			
5. "Problem" or "dysfunctional" students cannot learn responsibility and should be separated from "normal" students.			
6. A poor socioeconomic and family history make it impossible for a student to learn responsible behavior.			
7. Students should rely on extrinsic motivation to control their behavior.			
8. Teachers should reinforce acceptable student behavior with items exchangeable for privileges, fun activities, and events.			
9. Responsible students self-correct their behavior, use an internal locus of control, and accept the consequences of their behavior.			
10. Teachers should reward a student immediately and frequently, especially at the beginning when the student is becoming familiar with correct behavior.			
11. Only a small number of students in almost any classroom require serious attention for misbehavior.			
12. Teachers should model appropriate values and behavior.			
13. Teachers should use positive and negative reinforcements to modify the behavior of students within the classroom environment.			

Item	Rating		
	Agree	*Uncertain*	*Disagree*
14. Teachers should carefully monitor their own behavior in the classroom.			
15. Teachers should avoid correcting a misbehaving student to prevent damage to the student's self-esteem.			
16. When a student expresses dismay for being denied satisfaction of a demand, teachers should change their own behavior to meet the needs of the student.			
17. Teachers' guidance precludes students from experiencing the consequences of their behavior.			
18. Students should be allowed to experience the natural consequences of their behavior.			
19. An authoritarian approach to discipline permits a student to develop an internal locus of control.			
20. Teachers should not be concerned with developing democratic and multicultural values.			
21. Human equality, dignity, self-worth, and participation in decision making at all levels should be taught by teachers and integrated into the curriculum.			
22. The school and classroom environment are not important for developing a responsible student.			
23. A safe and inviting classroom is irrelevant to a student's success in school.			
24. Teachers should clearly state the objectives of their instruction.			
25. Teachers should praise students for exceptional performance.			
26. Teachers should not punish a student for misbehavior.			
27. Punishment and consequences are not the same.			

(Continued)

(Continued)

Item	Rating		
	Agree	*Uncertain*	*Disagree*
28. Encouragement and praise will have the same positive effects on a student's attitudes and behavior.			
29. A responsible student relies solely on external rewards to motivate learning.			
30. External rewards are essential tools in controlling student behavior.			
31. Teachers should not rely on strict rules to control a student's behavior.			
32. Expressing strong emotions when dealing with a student's classroom misbehavior effectively controls that behavior.			
33. Teachers should closely monitor students for conformance to a code of discipline.			
34. Students should be involved in the development of behavioral standards and guidelines.			
35. Teachers should eliminate negative consequences so that a student enjoys school.			
36. Students should question the rules established by the teacher or school.			
37. Within the context of the classroom, students should not be expected to derive solutions to problems based on their rational understanding of their inner selves.			
38. Responsible behavior must be constantly reinforced with external inducements.			
39. A responsible student has internalized acceptable standards of behavior.			
40. Forcing a student to behave allows the student to internalize acceptable standards of behavior.			
41. A student is usually unwilling to cooperate unless forced to do so.			

Item	Rating		
	Agree	*Uncertain*	*Disagree*
42. Students should take an active role in developing and implementing learning experiences in the classroom.			
43. The rational, inner self is a myth.			
44. Students should be taught to act autonomously.			
45. A teacher's demeanor has substantial effects on a student's behavior in the classroom.			
46. Teachers should not use popcorn, candy, or other enjoyable items to positively reinforce an appropriate behavior.			
47. Students should be permitted to experience the consequences of their behavior.			
48. Teachers should arrange rewards to increase acceptable behavior.			
49. When students are treated equally, they are always treated fairly.			
50. Teachers should reward desirable behavior often and lessen the rewards as the desirable behavior is expressed.			
51. Students require a sense of security and belonging to function in school effectively.			
52. Due to misbehavior, students must sometimes be physically removed from the classroom environment and placed in a time-out area.			
53. To control behavior, teachers should direct a student to repeat an unacceptable behavior until the student is unwilling to continue doing so.			
54. Teachers should provide incremental rewards for small and incremental improvements in behavior.			
55. Most students do not require strong disciplinary actions in the classroom.			

Key to The RCM Plan™ Inventory

Agree: 1, 3, 4, 9, 11, 12, 14, 18, 21, 24, 26, 27, 31, 34, 36, 39, 42, 44, 45, 46, 47, 51, 52, and 55.

Disagree: 2, 5, 6, 7, 8, 10, 13, 15, 16, 17, 19, 20, 22, 23, 25, 28, 29, 30, 32, 33, 35, 37, 38, 40, 41, 43, 48, 49, 50, 53, and 54.

LOOKING AHEAD

Chapter 1 presented a scenario similar to the real-life classrooms teachers must face daily, followed by a description of the traditional classroom plans that focus on external-control models, such as fears or bribes, in comparison to The RCMPlan™—a well-tested, internal-control model that allows students to correct undesirable behaviors. From here, the various roles and functions of the discipline review committee (DRC) were explained. Chapter 2 next presents procedures for setting up the instructional and classroom management environment.

CHAPTER TWO

Teaching Students Responsibility Within Warm and Inviting Classrooms

Parents can only give good advice or put them on the right paths, but the final forming of a person's character lies in their own hands.

—Anne Frank

LETTER TO DR. BROWN, MIDDLE SCHOOL METHODS

A first-year teacher writes to her former professor:

Dear Dr. Brown:

Is my life supposed to be like this? Yesterday, after teaching school all day, I found myself running out the door as the custodian was locking the building to leave. I was in a major panic as I suddenly realized that I

(Continued)

25

(Continued)

had spent the last hour comparing notes with colleagues to determine who has the worst-behaved kids and, as a result, left with today's lesson plans incomplete. As I carried twenty boxes of instructional materials to my car, I was mistaken for an employee of a major moving-van line.

Once I arrived at home, I prepared a seven-course dinner, cleaned the house, and got the children to bed before sitting down to reflect upon the day's events. I wondered why I had to tell Maurice three times to quit pulling the girls' hair. I even screamed at him one time. I felt guilty for losing my temper with him, and then later, I became furious with three girls who continued to whisper and were obviously making fun of Tonya, a girl not in "their group." I remember being in Tonya's shoes when I was their age. Middle school can be so cruel! Anyway, I was close to a nervous breakdown as I wondered what miracle I must perform to get Patrick to turn in his homework. I had three choices: either to crash on the bed in total exhaustion, complete tomorrow's lesson plans, or read the want ads for a new career in the morning's paper, which, by the way, was still unrolled. I crashed on the sofa before I could make the choice. Is this really what teaching is all about? Help!

Sincerely,
Jane D.

THE ORIGINAL AND STILL FUNCTIONAL CORRELATES FOR TEACHING RESPONSIBILITY

Jane should be able to relax. As explained in the Introduction and Chapter 1, The RCMPlan™ teaches students responsibility while effectively teaching them to manage their own behavior. To support this, we conducted a national study, and discovered the following correlates for responsible classroom management:

- Approximately 88 percent of students do not require a teacher's disciplinary action.
- Teachers, as responsible educators, can promote and assist students to be responsible.

- Any student can learn responsibility, regardless of family or socioeconomic limitations.
- Students can achieve higher levels of responsibility when teachers provide clear instructional objectives, use interactive methods of instruction, and set high expectations for appropriate behavior.
- Students can learn to resolve conflict and solve their own problems in a responsible manner.

EXPECTING RESPONSIBILITY AND CIVILITY IN THE CLASSROOM

One of RCM's basic premises is that students can learn responsibility. In order to promote student responsibility in the classroom, teachers must endorse the following principles:

- Classrooms are student centered.
- Instruction is active and exciting.
- Responsible behavior is learned and practiced.

A student-centered classroom is more of an educational philosophy than an educational term, but as we head into the second decade of the twenty-first century, this form of instruction is commonplace at all grade levels, K–12. However, at some point in America's history of education, the belief that student-centered instruction places less academic challenges upon the student developed. From our observations and our belief system, if done correctly, there is no approach to learning that is more rigorous than student-centered instruction. With student-centered instruction, the teacher discards the role of a passive content presenter. Instead, the teacher develops a motivating and academically challenging environment for students, where students actively explore and learn through interactive experiences. RCM embraces this environment: content is taught either directly or embedded within core curriculum to convey the concepts of personal responsibility. Responsibility must be learned before it can be practiced.

No longer does the teacher monitor structured, inflexible rules—rules that may not be appropriate or educationally sound. Instead, students learn to adapt to socially acceptable standards and guidelines. In The RCMPlan™, fairness is more important and effective than treating everyone the same. Student self monitoring, with necessary teacher guidance, leads to responsible students with responsible actions. What about behavior problems? This plan also provides instruction for effectively and successfully handling discipline problems.

At first glance, obedience is a positive concept. There is probably nothing wrong with wanting young people to be obedient. However, if adults use techniques for securing obedience improperly, or abusively force obedience upon an adolescent, he may respond negatively. Does a citizen pay taxes because it is the responsible thing to do? Or does a citizen pay taxes to avoid prison? Suffice it to say that people do some things out of obedience and are motivated to do other, more controllable, things by a sense of responsibility. The same is true for children. With greater autonomy, students can make responsible choices. As they internalize appropriate behavior, they should be allowed to experience consequences leading them to self-correct their behavior and become more responsible.

To achieve this sense of responsibility, the school and classroom climate should promote student ownership. Students should feel a sense of belonging through responsible decision making. For instance, faculty members who have input into schoolwide decisions feel a greater sense of ownership and self-worth than those mandated to obey the principal's directives. Many times, a student with difficulty controlling her behavior feels that all she receives are directives and limitations. Quite honestly, at times, this may be all this student can handle. Unfortunately, many of her actions occur in response to an external locus of control or are precipitated by a miscued internal reaction, such as attention deficit disorder or stabilization of medication. For example, the student may perform a task for a specified reward. However, if embarrassed or angered, she may rebel using inappropriate language, internalized from her environment, and disrupt classroom instruction. The teacher cannot meet the needs of this type of student while twenty-five others also expect instruction. Of greater importance, it is not fair to the teacher or the other students when a disruptive student interrupts their learning. The RCMPlan™provides guidance, with little emotional stress, for effectively managing this student.

Teaching Responsibility Directly

The instructional program at the middle and high school can include concepts about responsibility in numerous ways. Middle school teachers spend much time correlating and integrating instruction. They should not, then, find it too taxing to incorporate students' understanding of personal responsibility. Obviously, this is easier to incorporate in civics and other social sciences, as well as the sciences. In the high school, most disciplines can easily incorporate responsible and civil processes through instruction as students work in cooperative groups and share responsibilities. Teachers can illustrate how professionals in their disciplines all must be responsible in their fields, and how scientists, historians, writers, and business professionals practice responsibility and civility in their trades and as they work on their jobs. This discussion elicits many ideas. Others might include:

- Spend the first few days in all classes discussing various aspects of responsibility. For example, in the area of social studies at all grade levels, the concept of responsibility can be interwoven into almost any unit of study.
- Design an instructional bulletin board on responsible behavior to display students' drawings, cartoons, essays, etc.
- Invite students to write or draw ideas or concerns on a graffiti board.
- Assign students to write songs, poems, letters, and essays about responsibility, citizenship, and civility—worked into the current content.
- Ask students to relate to characters in textbook literature, novels, and short stories and identify concepts of responsibility, behavior, and consequences.
- Develop a "Wanted Poster" hall, bulletin board, or graffiti area, and allow students to write about what it means to be responsible students, good citizens, and/or productive members of society.
- Record student podcasts about responsible individuals studied in science or social studies.

- Develop a Wiki on a story the class has read and ask another class or school to collaborate with edits and changes.
- Create a blog about a responsible event in the community or state.
- Take on a grade-level or class special project for the American Heart Association or any nonprofit group and experience true responsibility through giving time and effort.

EXPERIMENTING WITH RESPONSIBILITY AND CIVILITY IN THE CLASSROOM

To address the need for responsibility and civility, educators can use students' social and personal interactions as instructional models. The classroom and school must be open, and a nurturing environment must prevail. Students will, in turn, learn to value personal relationships, as teachers emphasize caring for others in various learning situations. A student-centered school with school-spirit activities, and service projects in curriculum, will help achieve this: the school becomes a democratic community where students participate in decision making and feel free to express their opinions in a nonjudgmental atmosphere.

In a student-centered atmosphere, teachers equally provide attention, support, and encouragement to all students. Teachers achieve this by offering consistent encouragement during instructional activities, writing constructive comments on papers and projects, and circulating among students' desks to provide corrective comments during independent-work activities. With these practices, students are less likely to feel the need to speak out at inappropriate times. The high-level classroom monitoring helps alleviate classroom disruptions and promotes civil behaviors among students.

Role-playing activities provide strategies for students to handle themselves when challenging situations do occur. In these activities, students focus on how responsible and civil students handle conflict and problems in a socially acceptable manner. Role playing also illustrates how violating of a particular principle will be dealt with promptly, and how the violation will not be tolerated.

In conjunction with these strategies, RCM teachers emphasize cooperative-learning activities. With a number of opportunities to work and socialize in groups, teachers promote a high level of interaction. These practices also aid the development of effective communication and higher-level thinking skills, while promoting fellow students as resources. This emphasis also lessens competitiveness and the student comparisons of themselves with other students. In particular, Jigsaw II lessons and case method studies require more cooperation than most group activities and are not competitive in nature.

Teachers can also structure the classroom so that they and, on occasions, students, can act as role models in conflict situations. Defining expected behaviors and allowing time for students and the teacher to identify disruptive behaviors—to the class and the learning process—are effective means to achieve better student understanding. Taking the time to teach why certain behaviors are unacceptable and subsequently, as a class, developing a list of consequences for these behaviors, provides students with a sense of ownership. This helps students become even more responsible for their own behaviors.

Lessons enabling students to appreciate the importance of civility with other classmates further promote the development of responsible behavior. Teachers can share relevant literature focusing on these concepts, and the concepts can be included in most subject areas. Exposing students to behaviors demonstrating responsibility and civility makes the concepts relevant, and provides strategies for students to use them in their daily lives.

An emphasis on the importance of rights and responsibilities as part of the students' roles also fosters responsibility and civility. Whenever possible, teachers should allow students to resolve their own conflict. Teachers can ask questions to enable students to demonstrate understanding of what actually transpires during conflict situations or displays of inappropriate behavior. Students then begin to develop ways to better handle themselves and their behaviors.

It is also important for teachers to provide opportunities for students to demonstrate responsible behavior, such as assigning classroom chores or leadership positions. As a result, students learn to appreciate the value of intrinsic rewards and improve their self-concepts. Students feel better and are more conscious of how they treat others. With the development of these abilities, students also work harder and are more likely to give their personal best in all situations.

Attaining values of responsibility and civility can awaken the desire for knowledge, assist in the development of critical thinking, and promote an appreciation of accomplishments. Therefore, RCM classrooms must include life lessons that promote problem solving, social skills, and conflict resolution. Peer-mediation programs also enhance students' abilities to behave responsibly, due to an increased understanding of expectations and their own personal skills.

MODELING RESPONSIBLE BEHAVIOR

Students accept the values and emulate the behavior of people, such as teachers, who are important in their lives. As a responsible adult, a teacher consciously models values, attitudes, and behaviors that will lead a student to behave responsibly. Irresponsible adults model irresponsible behavior and often make decisions detrimental to themselves, as well as to students who depend on them for guidance. To be an effective, positive model, an RCM teacher must be a responsible adult. A responsible and competent teacher understands and skillfully practices the principles of student growth and development, and carefully monitors the quality of his own actions in guiding a student to responsible behavior.

In today's culture, parents and teachers often fear that they might damage a student's self-esteem merely by correcting unacceptable behavior. When a student expresses dismay because his demands were not met, the attending adult frequently responds with feelings of guilt. Rather than expect a change in the student's behavior, the adult alters her own behavior to avoid the student's unhappiness. The adult thus acts irresponsibly, forgetting the more important issue of providing guidance, and allowing the student's happiness to overshadow.

Guidance is essential to the development of a responsible student. Adults guide when they point in the direction of the desired behavior. When adults model important and desirable expectations for the community, they guide the student in becoming a successful member of the community. Importantly, guidance does not preclude a student from experiencing the consequences of exploration into acceptable and unacceptable behavior. By learning through honest mistakes and sometimes difficult experiences, a student will learn responsibility. By permitting students to safely experience the natural consequences of behavior, parents and teachers guide students appropriately and responsibly. By contrast, authoritarian or permissive forms of control often incite students to be uncooperative and belligerent; most critically, this allows little opportunity for students to internalize appropriate behavior.

Fairly Acknowledging Differences

Within the RCM classroom, individual students receive fair and equal, but not necessarily the same, treatment. Strict rules to obtain obedience insulate students from personal responsibility—a result contrary to RCM goals. When a student learns to act autonomously according to agreed-upon standards, the student acts responsibly. Responsible behavior does not require enforcement and repeats without applying external inducements. Accepting the premise that most students are naturally very honest, fair, and willing to cooperate, the RCM teacher uses natural and logical consequences to teach students to self-correct behavior. When a student internalizes the standards of behavior and becomes responsible, forcing a certain behavior is wholly unnecessary. In learning to act responsibly, a student simultaneously learns to be a productive member of the community. As a result, a responsible student is not a discipline problem.

The RCMPlan™ defines a classroom-management system that teaches students acceptable standards and guidelines for their behavior. RCM allows teachers to monitor and guide students in nurturing and accountable ways. With this, teachers have the independence to develop productive and stimulating classroom strategies to assist students with controlling their personal behavior. The RCMPlan™ motivates students to take an active role in developing and implementing classroom learning experiences. As students assume responsibility and accountability for their learning and self-discipline, they prepare for their future as mature and actively engaged adults.

Issues Affecting the Implementation of RCM

Prescribing who will be in any classroom is particularly difficult. Clearly, predicting that only 3 percent of any classroom will be dysfunctional is impossible. Also, the complexity of a student's background may be beyond the classroom teacher's skills and require a specialist's intervention. Of course, teachers must then be skilled and self-assured enough to recognize and properly deal with situations beyond their expertise. In some instances, even students engaged in only moderately problematic behavior cause serious difficulties for the unprepared teacher. When a student behaves disruptively and generates chaos, an unskilled teacher may lose an entire class.

In a less serious situation, teachers sometimes ignore those students who have withdrawn from normal interactions, but cause little classroom upheaval. These students act out their frustrations in a manner that they have found successful, but the indifferent teacher ultimately acts irresponsibly by leaving well enough alone.

Adults cannot always predict a student's behavior, and behavior may alter when family, school, or social conditions change. Even a responsible student may exhibit irresponsible behavior at times; it is the teacher's responsibility to skillfully guide a student to responsible behavior. If a teacher holds unrealistic expectations or poorly defines the expectations and, therefore, fails to provide realistic markers for responsible behavior, a student or even an entire classroom may lose their way and become a problem.

For the sake of order, predictability, and satisfying the needs of the greatest number, teachers sometimes rely on instructional models or formulas. These approaches delay the development of a student's sense of responsibility. Creativity, exploration, problem solving, and independent action diminish, resulting in bored and alienated students who seek stimulation through alternate and often undesirable means. By approaching instruction in such a manner, a teacher denies a fundamental principle of RCM and, more importantly, the dictates of human growth and development.

Practicing Internal-Behavior Control

Teachers often attempt to motivate students to learn and behave acceptably with external rewards. This process consumes a great deal of time and often results in students' sole reliance on extrinsic rewards to accomplish what should, instead, be intrinsically important to them. External rewards in the form of reinforcement or even the casual use of praise can be detrimental to the development of the responsible student.

The RCM approach to classroom management uses high expectations and reasonable guidelines and standards to develop intrinsic motivation. In the RCM classroom, teachers act swiftly, consistently, and unemotionally to effect desirable behavior. As students learn to internalize responsible behavior, their self-esteem matures, and they gain increasing control over their behavior.

Developing a Warm and Inviting Classroom

FOR REFLECTION

Take a minute to reflect upon the middle or high school that you attended as a student. What did you like about the school? Was it a warm, inviting place? If so, what made it inviting? If not, what made it uninviting? You can probably remember many characteristics of that school with great clarity and, if you were successful, as you obviously were, you recall mostly positive memories. If the memories are negative, you likely had tenacity and above-average intelligence allowing you to complete college, and perhaps graduate school, and embark upon a teaching career. Have you ever wondered what happened to some of the folks that dropped out of school? How about the students who sat in the back of the class? Do you ever wonder what happened to them? Does it make you angry that perhaps their parents and schools failed them? While teachers may have limited success working with parents of students like these in teaching responsibility, they have no excuse for not teaching responsibility in the nation's schools.

As explained in Chapter 1, the school and classroom environment, and the concomitant instructional effort, embody the RCM approach. In a safe and inviting environment, a student feels secure and protected, and is prepared to learn. The more positive the experience in the classroom, the greater the opportunity the teacher has to guide the students toward responsible behavior. The organization of space and time, the format and presentation of instructional materials, the demeanor of the teachers, and the amount and kind of preparation are all critically important to success in an environmentally sound school and classroom. RCM requires a teacher to clearly state the objectives of all planned classroom activity. This outcome-based approach to instruction necessitates the teacher's careful preparation and constant evaluation of student behavior. Precise and sensitive instructional guidance builds the foundation for responsible student behavior. When a teacher involves a student in a dynamic agenda, replete with value and purpose, the student will respond with certainty and optimism. As teachers elicit higher performance, students will not feel threatened, but rather motivated to meet their own standards. The RCM teacher encourages, and indeed, acknowledges exceptional performance and responsibility, but does not fall prey to using rewards and other forms of bribery to sustain the responsible student. An RCM teacher aims to avoid external rewards as a means to motivate student learning. Responsible students are intrinsically motivated students.

In designing a school environment to enhance student responsibility, all faculty and staff must endorse the three principles of a responsibility-oriented school environment.

1. Schools must be for students—not principals and not teachers.

2. Students must participate in the decisions made to keep their school safe, clean, and inviting.

3. School curricula must adequately place appropriate emphasis upon academics, problem solving, and responsibility.

Principals and teachers are very aware of the need for safe schools, but responding daily to inappropriate student misbehaviors is stressful and part of the teacher's job description. Principals get frustrated when teachers bring students to "the principal's office" for what is often viewed by school administrators as an insignificant reason. Multiply the event by a dozen or more daily, over a few weeks, and it does not take long for a beginning principal to become highly stressed and start directing teachers to take care of their own classroom management.

As a result, many principals distribute pages of quoted research on the high correlation of good teaching to lower incidences of classroom-management problems. A first-year principal gave the following account of a situation he faced after a few months in the position:

> I recall a stressed-out teacher, near tears, who came to my office for an administrative team meeting one day. I can't recall her major concerns, but she ended her tirade with, "I could get something done if it weren't for some of my students." It hadn't been a particularly good day for me either. Still in my infancy as a principal, I responded to her charge by saying, "I could get something done if it were not for some of my teachers."

Needless to say, both individuals were frustrated. Perhaps their stress occurred because their needs were not being met. While the problem may arise from differences in perception and communication, or the lack of an effective classroom-management plan that clearly differentiates between acts of school violence and lost homework, the stress still exists—thus the need for a program such as RCM to avoid such problems. Yet, educators must recognize that addressing their own needs is secondary to addressing those of students. Unfortunately, we have experienced teachers and principals who act as though they have the deed of the school in their pocket, and act as though their needs are the priority. It is easy to forget that we, as educators, must always be in the adult mode and genuinely believe that schools are for students. Educators are employees and if anyone owns the schools, it must be the students. Schools administrators, teachers, and other staff members who believe differently have great difficulty in successfully meeting the academic, social, physical, and developmental outcomes central to the purpose of schools.

Effective schools are safe. With increased violence in American society and in schools, feeling safe can be difficult. Potentially disruptive students cannot be locked out of the building; however, several safety precautions can be implemented. Teachers can do the following:

- Report any unidentified person on the school grounds to the office, and teach students to inform adults if they see anyone or anything out of the ordinary. (Visitors should wear an official badge or a hold a visitor's pass.)
- Teach students safety procedures for any item from cutting instruments in sixth grade to using candles while conducting science experiments in the fifth grade, and remember to review these procedures at regular intervals.
- Review and practice fire, tornado, and other emergency drills and procedures on a regular basis.
- Integrate teaching safe habits into all areas of the instructional program, not just into health classes.
- Encourage the district administration to work with other local agencies to provide crossing guards, school police officers, and school nurses for all schools.

"Cleanliness is next to godliness" goes the saying. Sometimes, getting students to take a bath can be difficult. The same goes for getting students to clean up their work spaces at school. However, with a little teacher coaxing and reinforcement, tasks are accomplished. While teaching cleanliness should start at home, it is not that students lack knowledge of good hygiene and cleanliness, but rather that they lack respect for themselves, the school, or both. How can principals and teachers instill in students personal dignity for themselves and respect for school property?

Perhaps the first thing a school can do is establish a beautification committee. To maximize success, consider the following:

- Include a school administrator, teachers, students, parents, and the head custodian on the committee.
- Allow students to directly participate in decisions made about the school environment. School beautification contests can solicit ideas from classes and individual students, with the best suggestions recognized and then implemented via leadership from the classes and students who proposed them. All classes should be encouraged and expected to participate.
- Hold PTA or booster club fundraisers to replace unsightly or damaged playground equipment, or to plant trees, bushes,

and flowers. If maintenance funding within the school system is limited, PTA members can initiate a classroom-repainting project. Whatever the need may be, at all costs, students should be directly involved—from planning stages through full implementation.

- At all grade levels, hold students accountable for maintaining neat and clean desks and lockers. Students can clean classrooms and surrounding areas on a weekly schedule, including straightening materials and replacing misplaced items; dusting and washing desks, tables, and equipment in the room; and discarding clutter accumulated during the week. Students enjoy decorating and personalizing their space, and should be encouraged to act on their ideas. Clubs, grade levels, and classes can also form teams to plan and share their ideas for cleaning and beautification under appropriate supervision.

- Place custodial staff on a shift schedule. This is a common approach in the business community, due to difficulty cleaning a building during the hours of operation. School administration can schedule at least two custodial shifts. For example, minimal custodial support would occur during the school day for duties that must be performed at that time. The next shift of custodians would clean the building after school. At the system level, this concept can expand to include custodial teams who clean several schools a day after operating hours.

By following some of these recommendations, schools can maintain a safe and clean environment. However, this alone is not enough. Schools must also be inviting. Of course, a safe and clean school is more inviting than an unsafe or unclean school. Yet, not all safe and clean places are inviting. Everyone has eaten in a clean and safe restaurant, but where they still felt out of place. How about a bank, a retail store, or a health club? If people feel out of place and unwelcome, they usually do not go back. They have an option. Students, on the other hand, do not have the option to not return to an uninviting school. If given a choice, students would elect to attend the school where they feel most comfortable, accepted, and invited. Until students gain that option, educators must work collaboratively with students to make the school environment more inviting. This requires a commitment at the classroom level and at the school level.

To develop a more inviting atmosphere, schools can take inventory of ideas at a staff meeting to make the school more inviting—for faculty and staff as well as students. If the principal requests ideas and faculty members don't respond, he could consider that he may stand in the way of a warmer environment. With only the risk of a few ego bruises, and without losing authority, he could then initiate healthy changes. As researchers and former school leaders, we have found the best way to improve morale and make a more inviting work environment is to *empower responsible teachers to make responsible decisions*.

THE FOUR TYPES OF INVITING TEACHERS

Much of what is inviting for teachers is also inviting for students. Just as a staff wants input on ways a school can be made more inviting, so does the student population. How can students learn responsibility and democracy if they are not allowed to be involved in the decision-making process? Our vast experience working with students reveals that students do have this ability and they are not inclined to abuse this right; the practice also supports the principles of true democracy. To further illustrate this process, William Purkey (1989), recently retired professor from UNC Greensboro and cofounder of the Alliance for Invitational Education, identifies the four types of invitations teachers give to students: (1) An intentionally disinviting teacher goes out of the way to make students feel uninvited (least effective and most detrimental). (2) An unintentionally disinviting teacher carelessly ignores or does not pay attention or seize opportunities. (3) An intentionally inviting teacher works hard to design and implement plans so that all students feel invited. (This teacher is often seen as fake or not real.) (4) An inherently inviting teacher allows all students to learn and to feel ownership (most effective). While we present Purkey's categories in a different order and perhaps in a different hierarchy from other writers, we believe this classification best aligns with The RCMPlan™.

Another component of a safe and inviting environment "invites" teachers and staff to dress professionally. In turn, teachers encourage and recognize appropriate dress for students. We believe that students show a greater respect for a teacher who dresses as a responsible educator.

PREPARING TO MODIFY CLASSROOM PROCEDURES

In replacing school rules with standards and guidelines, The RCMPlan™ may, at first, shock students, but they quickly adjust. Students view regulations and rigid rules as uninviting and as a result, frequently break them. Rules demand obedience. Rules do not foster building responsibility; rather, they dictate external control. Standards and guidelines, on the other hand, provide opportunity to address situational differences with flexibility. Some situations, of course, require obedience, but rules do not always promote a student's well-being because they enforce inflexibility or conformity. In contrast to rules, standards and guidelines allow students ownership of their own behavior. Standards and guidelines permit responsibility as students experience a self-correcting, logical consequence.

Some students may have difficulty adjusting to this because they have always been forced to be obedient; they have never been allowed to be responsible. For these students, the teacher may initially alter the approach from a collaborative one to a more external-controlling environment until the students establish a more internal understanding that fosters responsible behavior.

FOR REFLECTION

If you were to write down a description of the best teachers you had while in middle or high school, you would most likely include the teachers who cared for you as a person and who made learning exciting. You may not remember all of the algebra, French, or geography taught, but you do remember the excitement and joy of being part of that particular class. Even a lecture can be active if effectively delivered.

STUDENT ROLES AND ADDITIONS TO THE CLASSROOM

Arranging the classroom in an attractive, warm, and inviting manner before students arrive assists in teaching responsibility. Bulletin boards can display the work of last year's students in a proud and boastful manner. Contrary to straight rows, chairs, tables, and desks can be arranged so that all students can easily see each other.

Once students arrive, teachers can boost creativity by periodically eliciting students' input for changing the structure. Younger students will need more guidance in the beginning and their arrangements may be unusual, to say the least. However, if teachers don't allow students to make these decisions, how can students learn to care for the classroom?

Student artwork displayed throughout the classroom adds warmth, and teachers can bring a few nice plants from home and encourage students to do the same. In addition, students maintain a sense of home by keeping selected personal items on their desks, such as picture of a favorite pet or a teenage idol. Since students spend half of their waking hours at school, classrooms must belong to the kids.

Complementing the physical environment, teachers can greet students in a caring and loving manner. A statement such as, "Hi, Sasha. I'm glad you are here today. I have an exciting experiment for us to do on . . . " or "a story about . . . " or "a game . . . " surely invites a successful day. Students often talk about how they love the first day of school. Educators can sustain this attitude through the remaining 179 days. If every day had the excitement of the first day, there would be few school problems. While everybody has good and bad days, anyone can manage a smile and a pleasant greeting. If every student has a teacher who says to them, every day, "I'm glad you are here today," what an inviting world the schools would become. There would be limited behavior problems. There would be more respect for teachers. Authority is given, but respect must be earned. Educators who forget this basic premise are doomed to fail, and so are their students.

RCM teachers interact with their students and get to know them. They assertively become informed about students' personal lives. When teachers ask the right questions, the most they will have to do is to listen. Teachers can also consider sharing a little of their personal selves on a regular basis. While, in recent decades, direct conversational time between students and adults on a daily basis has dropped dramatically, recounting an experience in the grocery store or a predicament a son experiences shows students that a teacher's life does not revolve solely around the classroom.

As teachers talk with students, they can suggest multiple avenues to explore in solving problems or investigating ideas—a positive component of the learning process. By avoiding preaching and excessive correctives, teachers instead teach by example.

The student subsequently learns that the teacher cares for the student as a "whole being."

Students and youth, if they haven't been developmentally damaged, possess a natural propensity for truth and fairness. Caring teachers, then, will easily gain their respect. With this respect, major behavior problems are unlikely. However, teachers must keep in mind that they need not be personal friends or buddies to earn respect. In fact, this potentially damages the integrity of the relationship. Respect derives simply from doing the things a caring teacher does—knowing when to reprimand, to hug, to counsel, and to listen. Occasionally, educators make mistakes. This is natural. Students forgive more when they know the mistakes are not intentional and the mistakes are acknowledged. Everyone makes mistakes as they grow. Stagnation is not growth.

Teachers can design classroom environments to teach and reinforce responsible behaviors daily. Daily discussions depicting responsible behavior show students the many ways this can look. One definition is behavior that demonstrates a value of the principles of honesty, morality, and commitment. A responsible person is accountable for his actions and accepts that with any action, there is a natural consequence.

Responsible behavior begins at home as students learn by modeling their parents. Students chart their futures according to the resolution of early conflicts. Whether teachers assist or hinder a student's efforts to resolve these conflicts and develop responsible behavior depends on how they model responsible behavior to students, and how they monitor socially appropriate and inappropriate behavior with respect to standards and guidelines.

GROUP ACTIVITIES

1. Individually, design a lesson to help teach the concept of responsibility that is embedded within a topic or specific lesson in a subject area. Share copies of this "lesson plan" with other teachers at your grade level or in your subject areas. Take a chance and really think outside of the box. As a group, take all of the lessons to a session conducted by the principal and DRC members, scheduled early in The RCMPlan™ staff development.

2. After the introductory session on The RCMPlan™, and after reading Chapters 1 and 2, start a personal journal to record your feelings about the changes that will occur with the new model. Along with this, list successes and failures over the next few months and, if you feel comfortable, share some of the positive and negative points you have made with a DRC member.

3. Either in grade-level teams or subject area groups, list the physical changes that could be made to the school and/or specific classrooms, lunchroom, and playground to make the total environment more "inviting" to students.

4. Discuss how these changes would also make the school more inviting to teachers.

5. Prepare a list of these changes for the principal or a DRC member.

6. As often as possible, review the RCM inventory at the end of Chapter 1 to make sure you remain consistent with the model.

7. Discuss steps that would be needed to start a grade level, department, or schoolwide beautification committee with your students. How could this be turned into part of an instructional unit or service project? To receive and share ideas with other teachers throughout the country, visit The RCMPlan™ Web site (www.rcmplan.com).

LOOKING AHEAD

This chapter presented instruction for setting up an inviting environment, with a few ideas to start incorporating concepts of responsibility and civility into the already existing curriculum. Teachers and staff are now be ready to begin developing school and classroom standards, guidelines, and expected behaviors. This is the focus of Chapter 3.

CHAPTER THREE

Standards, Guidelines, and Expected Behaviors

Individual commitment to a group effort—that is what makes a team work, a company work, a society work, a civilization work.

—Vince Lombardi

WHY RULES DO NOT WORK WITH MIDDLE OR SECONDARY SCHOOL STUDENTS

Before additional information is presented, take a few moments to answer the following questions with "yes" or "no":

_____1. While driving on the highway, have you ever traveled more than the posted speed limit?

_____2. In school, did you ever cheat on an exam or schoolwork?

_____3. On your taxes, did you ever fail to report money you earned that was paid to you in cash?

_____4. While employed as a teacher, have you ever taken or used school property for personal use?

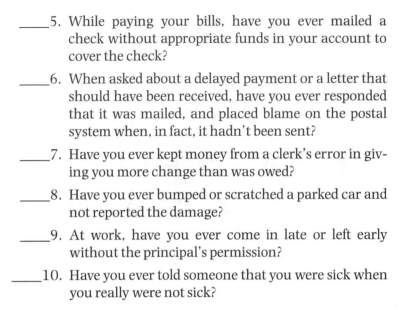

_____5. While paying your bills, have you ever mailed a check without appropriate funds in your account to cover the check?

_____6. When asked about a delayed payment or a letter that should have been received, have you ever responded that it was mailed, and placed blame on the postal system when, in fact, it hadn't been sent?

_____7. Have you ever kept money from a clerk's error in giving you more change than was owed?

_____8. Have you ever bumped or scratched a parked car and not reported the damage?

_____9. At work, have you ever come in late or left early without the principal's permission?

_____10. Have you ever told someone that you were sick when you really were not sick?

While answers of "yes" to any of these questions may not label one as a convict, there is a point to be made. Although most people have broken some of the rules, most people are basically moral individuals. Then why are rules broken? Better still, when are rules broken? As members of society, individuals break rules when they think the rules are senseless or inappropriate. People break rules when they are either in need or have a limited fear of getting caught. For example, Mr. Smith leaves work late and needs to get home. He sees no highway patrol officers so he exceeds the speed limit to make up for lost time. Another example might be when he goes to the movies instead of completing the unpleasant task of scoring the sixty essays, which he promised to return the next day, and then tells his students a brief illness prevented him from finishing.

Responsibility can be measured by degree. For instance, if someone answered "no" to all of the above questions, he may be viewed as more responsible than someone who answered only five of the ten questions with a negative response. Actions directly relate to how one measures right and wrong. Value structure directs one's level of responsibility.

The Limitations of Rules

Rules, whether written or implied, place restraints on individuals as members of a free society. They establish boundaries, and boundaries are important. With no boundaries, chaos results. Students and youth need boundaries, also. Without healthy boundaries, students do not feel safe nor do they develop normally. However, rules are absolute. Rules imply rigidity and equal treatment. They don't accommodate for individual differences or recognize that everyone is not equal.

Many students learn to follow the rules as long as the authority figure is monitoring. Some students actively resist an environment alien to their way of life, or that cannot accommodate their individual differences without judgment. Sometimes teachers bribe students into achieving or behaving. In all of these situations, these students learn externally enforced obedience that does not teach a true sense of responsibility.

Responsible Teaching

Responsible teachers relay discipline through teaching and practice, while promoting students' internal responsibility, accommodating their individual differences, and respecting their dignity as human beings. Teachers can learn to discipline with respect and without the overemphasized fear that curbs the positive development of a student's self-esteem.

In order for teachers to effectively teach responsibility to students, they, themselves, must be responsible adults. This is paramount to the success of this program. Therefore, to properly implement The RCMPlan™, teachers may have to modify some of their teaching behaviors. The major behaviors a successful teacher must practice are as follows:

- Replace school and classroom rules with standards and guidelines.
- Use expected behaviors based upon standards and guidelines to teach desirable student behaviors.
- Expect responsible behavior from all students in the school, and not just in one's own classroom.

Teachers who have focused classroom management on rules will find that using standards, guidelines, and expected behaviors makes student management more effective and less stressful; it results in responsible students who grow up to be responsible adults.

REPLACING RULES WITH SCHOOL AND CLASSROOM STANDARDS, GUIDELINES, AND EXPECTED BEHAVIORS

The RCMPlan™ does not use rules. Instead, teachers use standards, guidelines, and directives. Standards define the general direction of the responsible behavior. Example: "I am responsible for all of my actions." Guidelines provide specific guidance toward successfully meeting those standards. Example: "I will follow the teacher's directions." Expected behaviors offer specific statements for desired student actions. Example: "I will have all my homework completed and on my desk at start of algebra class."

Standards

Cooperatively designed by faculty and staff, standards formalize behavior and academic expectations. Some examples of standards are as follows:

- I am responsible for all of my actions.
- My success directly relates to my effort.
- To achieve in life, I must obtain an education.

These are just a few examples. However, the school and classroom should keep the number to a minimum of three. We recommend one overall standard for the entire school and all classrooms.

The School and Classroom Standard: "I Am Responsible for My Actions."

By far, the most effective schools have used only one standard for the entire school. Exceedingly, the most successful standard states, "I am responsible for all my actions [at Smith Middle or High School.]" Standards work in conjunction with guidelines, discussed in detail in the proceeding section, but also essential for understanding standards, because guidelines provide direction and align directly with the standard. Younger students will need more input from the teacher to understand guidelines than older students. In either case, the teacher ensures that the guidelines are educationally sound and fair, but some schools allow students to assist teachers in developing classroom standards and guidelines. In the middle or secondary schools, school and classroom standards and guidelines are most effective when developed by subject or grade-level teams of teachers. By far, most schools use grade-level teams.

Classroom and school standards may or may not be the same. However, the classroom program incorporates the school standard, practiced schoolwide. In fact, the most successful schools use *only one* standard for the school and all of the classrooms. ("I am responsible for all of my actions.") One core standard is less confusing to students and staff, and enables teachers to assure that standards are followed consistently. Again, no more than three standards should be used on a schoolwide or classroom basis. To reiterate, we find that, by far, most effective schools employ only one schoolwide standard encompassing the basic desire of school stakeholders.

Guidelines

While the standard is an overall general statement of desired behavior, the guideline(s) define the educators' desires and intentions in more concrete terms. Classroom guidelines provide more specific direction, while expected behaviors illustrate the guideline in action for individual grade levels or individual classrooms. In the most successful middle and secondary schools using The RCMPlan™, the entire school has *one standard* and *three or four guidelines*. The standard and related guidelines are all the same throughout the school, but expected behaviors are designed to be developmentally appropriate for grade levels in the middle or high school. While the school standard must be visibly posted throughout the school, the classroom standard and guidelines must be posted at a major focal point in the classrooms. Some schools professionally paint the standard—and in some cases, the standard and guidelines—on some of the school's entrance walls and in each classroom.

Both middle schools and high schools usually have schoolwide guidelines for hall, lunchroom, and bus behaviors, while high schools often include guidelines for safe driving on campus and for appropriately displaying affection. Student guidelines always apply for the classrooms as well as any additional classroom guidelines. Unlike classroom guidelines, school guidelines take the specific role of expected behaviors and there is only one (schoolwide) consequence for breaking the guideline. In this case, usually the observing teacher takes the student to a homeroom teacher, the office, or ICU (discussed later in this chapter).

Expected Behaviors

Derived directly from guidelines, expected behaviors specify daily actions based on grade level. For example, while every grade level may hold the guideline, "I will come to school prepared to learn," the expected behaviors would differ for sixth graders and tenth graders. Expected behaviors demonstrate the expected class procedures for each student at each level. While some students figure out the expected behaviors on their own, many students will need to learn them; regardless, these should be always reviewed.

RCM POINT 1

For the best results, use one standard for the school and classrooms and no more than three guidelines with three correlating expected behaviors. The most prevalent standard with examples of the most common guideline and expected behaviors are as follows:

Standard for the school and all classrooms: I am responsible for my actions.

Guideline 1 in tenth grade classrooms: I come to school prepared and ready to learn.

Expected behavior for **Guideline 1**: I will come to school with a positive attitude and ready to learn, with all assignments completed and with all my materials (books, notebook, pencil, and paper) with me for immediate use.

RCM POINT 2

Technically, when a student breaks an **expected behavior,** the related **guideline** is also broken; therefore, the student also breaks the **standard.** In the tenth grade example in RCM Point 1, if a student breaks the expected behavior, "I am to have my homework complete and ready to review at the beginning of geometry class," the student also breaks the guideline, "I will come to school prepared and ready to learn." Therefore, the student also breaks the standard, "I am responsible for my actions." A responsible student simultaneously follows standards, guidelines, and expected behaviors. Once a student understands this, responsible behavior begins to internalize; when all students reach this point, mass academic and behavioral changes are readily observed.

BUILDING SCHOOL GUIDELINES FOR OUTSIDE THE CLASSROOM

For the best results, educators (usually class or subject representatives or the discipline review committee) collaborate to develop *one* major schoolwide standard that also serves as the classroom standard. Next, the group develops other school guidelines for areas outside of the classroom walls, such as the lunchroom, media center, and hallways. At the high school level, these discussions should include issues such as driving privileges and leaving campus for labs or other classes, and also guidelines for appropriate personal and intimate contact. Once the DRC further reviews and approves these guidelines, the faculty at large grant final approval. Before implementation, the DRC chair and school principal review all outside guidelines approved by the faculty, and check for board policy to identify any conflicts or state-law concerns. Once approved by the principal, the DRC finalizes the school standard and guidelines.

Middle schools may have fewer classroom guidelines than high schools. Some schools use guidelines and expected behaviors for outside of the classroom related to hall and lunchroom behaviors. An example of an expected behavior for everyone is,

"All students walk in the halls at all times." A few schools also use these schoolwide expected behaviors for the bus and gym. Usually, stated consequences are determined by the faculty and/or the DRC and are included within the plan. Of course, principals approve these guidelines; they are taught to students, and also placed in a teacher handbook and the student guide.

At the middle and high school level, some outside guidelines and expected behaviors are the same or very similar. It is important to always consider civility in these guidelines, especially for students in sixth through tenth grade. Some students, especially middle school girls, can be quite brutal in their comments to certain classmates. With boys, it is often more physical, but this has changed in some locations throughout the country.

DEVELOPING CLASSROOM GUIDELINES

While the classroom teacher oversees classroom guidelines, it is more productive for grade-level teams to design these guidelines. For example, the team could develop, "I will come to school prepared and ready to learn." From here, individual or team expected behaviors evolve. Special area and specific grade-level teachers can then establish their own guidelines and expected behaviors, or use or adapt the grade-level teams' guidelines and behaviors. For consistency, the DRC then approves all guidelines and expected behaviors.

Classroom guidelines are posted in the class, and taught to the students with discussion and role playing as necessary. For example, the guideline, "I will come to school prepared and ready to learn," will have different expectations for sixth grade students than for twelfth grade students. When possible, it is beneficial to positively phrase the standard, guidelines, and expected behaviors. Standards and guidelines always emphasize "I," and more effectively, also include a goal, such as, "To be a responsible student in tenth grade, *I* will. . . ."

School Standard
As a student at Smith Middle School (or Queen Senior High School), I am responsible for all of my actions.

School Guideline

Any serious or repetitive act of student behavior that disrupts the normal educational process is considered irresponsible behavior.

Sixth Grade Guidelines

To be responsible in sixth grade math class (or Mrs. Willis's math class), I will . . .

1. Respect myself, other students, and school property.

2. Put forth my best effort with a positive attitude.

Ninth Grade Guidelines

To be responsible in ninth grade civics' class, I will . . .

1. Come to class with appropriate materials and prepared to learn.

2. Participate in class activities with a positive attitude.

Nationally, at all school levels, by far the most successful plans incorporate the following schoolwide standards and guidelines:

School and Classroom Standard

I am responsible for all my actions.

School and Classroom Guidelines

I will come to school prepared and ready to learn.

I will follow the directions from my teacher and any other adult working in the school.

I will respect myself and practice responsibility and civility with my classmates.

Classroom Expected Behaviors

These are usually two or three specific behaviors based on each of the presented guidelines and, for developmental purposes, are developed by grade-level teams. For example, coming to school prepared and ready to learn means something quite different for seventh grade math students than for tenth grade algebra students.

MAJOR POINT 3

Nationally, for middle or secondary schools, the most successful plan—exceedingly—is a very simple model. In this RCMPlan™, the middle or secondary school chooses one standard for both the school and the classroom, and three or four guidelines for special areas outside of the school. While the school standard also serves as the classroom standard, all students and faculty members understand the school guidelines—each with the specific consequence. Grade-level or subject teams build their own guidelines, with specific and developmentally appropriate expected behaviors. Classroom teachers handle their own students who break expected behaviors *when in class*. Outside of the classroom, when school guidelines are violated, the observing teacher follows the school consequence approved for The RCMPlan™ at the school. For example, if a student runs in the hall and this breaks a school guideline, the teacher nearest to the student is charged with implementing the school consequence.

School and Classroom Standard

At Smith City Middle School, I am responsible for all my actions.

School Guidelines

I will walk at a normal pace in the hall.

I will avoid using a loud voice or screaming anywhere outside of the classroom.

I will keep my personal locker clean and in order at all times.

Classroom Guidelines

I will come to school prepared and ready to learn.

I will follow the directions from my teacher and any other adult working in the school.

I will respect myself and practice responsibility and civility with my classmates.

School and Classroom Expected Behaviors

These are usually two or three specific requirements for classroom use.

An example of an expected behavior for classroom Guideline 1 for ninth grade students

> I will bring all required books, class materials, calculators, and homework to class.

An example for Guideline 2

> I will follow the directions from my teachers without question or comment.

TEACHING STANDARDS AND GUIDELINES TO STUDENTS

As discussed in Chapter 2, students must learn responsible behavior before they are held accountable. While suggestions in this book effectively support teaching overall concepts of responsibility, all classroom teachers must instruct all students in the standard, guidelines, and expected behaviors using appropriate language and activities for each grade level. Teachers can demonstrate appropriate behaviors and then students can emulate the desired behavior. Teachers can also provide a role-playing scenario. Older students problem solve inappropriate situations and behaviors in cooperative groups, and then role play both the negative and the desirable actions.

In all of these activities, teachers can easily observe the actual activity or review written results to assess students' outcomes. Furthermore, teachers can directly ask students questions to gauge understanding, and then monitor improvement by continuing these questions at the beginning of subsequent activities. What are the standards, guidelines, and expected behaviors? Again, the student guide should include all standards, guidelines, outside behaviors, grade-level guidelines and expected behaviors. Likewise, a teacher handbook and/or staff guide should include all procedures for RCM.

LOOKING AHEAD

This chapter outlined standards, guidelines, and expected behaviors. The RCMPlan™ is now ready for implementation. The next steps develop a large pool of consequences to correct inappropriate behavior and teach students to become more responsible. Chapter 4 explains how consequences, the intensive care unit, and the behavior improvement plans help students correct undesirable behavior.

CHAPTER FOUR

Using Consequences to Teach Responsibility

I believe that we are solely responsible for our choices, and we have to accept the consequences of every deed, word, and thought throughout our lifetime.

—Elisabeth Kübler-Ross

USING LOGICAL CONSEQUENCES VERSUS PUNISHMENT

The RCMPlan™ strongly emphasizes responsible behavior for responsible people in a responsible society. If all educators embrace this approach, the vast majority of students will exhibit appropriate behaviors. Teachers with the best results establish and maintain positive and developmentally appropriate expectations. Teaching then becomes a joy again.

Based on our research experience, 88 percent of students need very little to no corrective action. For the 9 percent who need some minor behavior changes, and the most difficult 3 percent who require increased correction, what can teachers do? If teachers implement The RCMPlan™ as stated so far, students requiring disciplinary action may not be as high as 12 percent. However, a better answer to the question is for teachers to permit the occurrence of logical consequences for students who have difficulty adhering to standards, guidelines, and expected behaviors.

All students will occasionally need reminders to correct behavior. However, the responsible student will develop an internal locus of control, allowing him to develop self-correcting mechanisms. Sometimes, the student with a minor problem simply needs someone to listen and to offer guidance. Many times, teachers work well with the student who needs only occasional redirection. However, teachers may not work as effectively with the student who has chronic behavior problems. Yet, a teacher still must work with *all* students and, therefore, develop strategies for *all* students to avoid the major pitfalls that can hinder success. Before using logical consequences with students for inappropriate behavior, the teacher must review her own role in the current situation. The following actions can create or exacerbate student-teacher conflict:

- promising students rewards for completed tasks
- arguing about a problem with a student of any age
- becoming emotional when correcting students
- raising voice level above normal range
- praising students when praise is undeserved
- giving rewards to obtain appropriate behavior
- embarrassing or belittling students
- using inappropriate language with students (i.e., shut up, dumb, pathetic)
- treating students unfairly
- planning ineffectively for instruction

These are the most serious, and most common, pitfalls to The RCMPlan™ inherent in teacher-student conflicts. When a teacher commits one or more of these common pitfalls, both the student and the teacher suffer. Fear of punishment or threat of coercion can achieve some degree of obedient behavior or short-range control, but it is temporary and ineffective in teaching responsibility. It is sad to hear a teacher boast that he has punished a student for inappropriate behavior. He may have eliminated the behavior problem for a short time, but, illogically, he probably lost the student. Teachers must manage student behavior and respect the individual student's self-esteem—balancing the two. Teachers have a right and a responsibility to teach. Students have a right to an education, but a responsibility not to interfere with the learning of other students. Teachers can easily avoid these conflicts by remaining responsible and professional. Most of the teacher-student conflicts listed are self-explanatory; however, here are elaborations for several scenarios:

- *A threatening teacher who shouts to maintain order easily intimidates some students.* These students may never feel any partnership or ownership in their class because they constantly guard for an attack from the teacher. In order to work to their potential, students must feel at ease. To effectively manage student behavior, the teacher must feel at ease with her authority in the classroom.
- *When a teacher argues with the students, both teacher and students lose.* A teacher does not need to argue, or tolerate unacceptable behavior. Arguing with a student does not improve unacceptable behavior. It may only place the teacher within the control of the student. Older students will do almost anything, including arguing, to avoid losing face among their peers. Nobody wins in this situation.
- *Bored or confused students create more problems within the classroom.* Implementing active instructional strategies and including interactive activities in the instructional program reduces the majority of behavior problems in the classroom. Students who are motivated and engaged in their learning have little time for misbehavior. They also have much greater respect for the teacher. Highly respected teachers have few behavior problems at any grade level or in any subject.
- *Teachers who use rewards as bribery or promise rewards for good behavior thwart development of responsibility.* This

external-controlling mechanism focuses student attention on gaining the reward, not on establishing responsible behavior. Students become dependent upon rewards as an external stimulation to accomplish a task. The effects of rewards are only short-lived and do not encourage responsible performance without a repeat of the reward. Teachers should instead encourage, acknowledge, and affirm student achievement and appropriate behavior.

What should teachers do when students do not follow the standard, and break guidelines by not following expected behaviors? First, teachers can limit the opportunity for the behavior to reoccur and allow the student to experience the logical consequences.

Assigning Consequences According to the Degree of Inappropriate Behavior

Logical consequences link the student's inappropriate action to a specific guideline and expected behavior. Logical consequences are not punishment. These actions result naturally from not doing what is expected. For example, one guideline states, "The student is to come to school prepared to learn." In discussing expectations for this guideline, the teacher directs students to complete a specific homework assignment. Every student is to do the homework. If a student comes in without her homework, she is not threatened with a low grade. Instead, she is asked when she would like to complete the assignment—at break, during lunch, or after school. Those are her choices. What happens if she doesn't have her homework in the future? The same or a similar consequence is used. In another example, a student throws food in the cafeteria. A logical consequence is for the student to sit by the teacher or alone until he chooses to act responsibly in the cafeteria. Only a rebellious student will create a scene over the enforcement of this logical consequence.

In another example, a student breaks a school guideline by throwing food in the cafeteria. The logical consequence, specifically developed with The RCMPlan™, is for the nearest teacher to remove the student from the lunchroom and take the student to ICU. Only a rebellious student will create a scene over the enforcement of this logical consequence. By rebelling, the student breaks another guideline—one that requires students to follow teacher directions. Even if no such guideline exists, the standard, "I am responsible for my actions," would still be broken.

The setting for permitting a logical consequence should be private, personalized, and professional. For example, when a teacher and student discuss the consequences of not doing her homework, the teacher should show no emotional reaction—either verbally or nonverbally. Sometimes a student has a reasonable explanation for a certain behavior. The teacher should always listen to the reason, and identify patterns. For instance, a teacher requires all students going on a class field trip to return a permission form signed by a parent/guardian. On the day of the field trip, a sixth grader has not returned the permission form given to him three days earlier. He explains that his mother signed it and inadvertently placed it in her briefcase. His mother is out of town on a business trip, but calls the teacher long distance at the last minute and explains the situation. What will most teachers do? Will the student be held accountable and not allowed to go? Or will the teacher vary the consequence? Before a teacher finalizes the consequence, she may want to consider the following questions: Did she give adequate time to return the signed permission? Consequences should be reasonable and fair for the student at the particular age and stage of development. Remember, a consequence that works for one student may not work for another student.

While a student shouldn't be penalized for the actions of his parents, the teacher does the students no favors when overlooking actions that are well within his control. In this case, the students had three days to return the form. A logical consequence would be to miss the field trip, and thus correct the behavior. The student will not forget the form in the future.

DEVELOPING A POOL OF CONSEQUENCES FOR SELECTIVE USE IN THE CLASSROOM

Teachers should have several consequences available for any inappropriate action. The more logical consequences available, the more effectively the teacher can address any specific situation. *Being fair to students doesn't always mean treating students the same.* Every situation is different. Students come from a variety of backgrounds and situations. Where one student receives a consequence for a behavior over which she has control, that same consequence may be inappropriate for a student with more control. Most inappropriate behavior can be measured in degrees, as can appropriate, logical consequences.

What if a student becomes hostile or refuses to accept the consequences of his action or continues to experience ineffective consequences? That student may need to be temporarily removed from the class and placed in time-out or, if severe, in intensive care.

Teaming With Other Teachers to Address Out-of-Classroom Infractions

As explained in Chapter 3, all teachers must assist in monitoring The RCMPlan™ outside of their classrooms. For example, a sixth grade teacher must confront two eighth grade students running in the hall or fighting outside. The DRC leads the faculty in developing the exact procedures. Does the teacher verbally reprimand the students, take them to ICU, or walk them to the homeroom teacher? These determinations are essential; plans for handling student misbehavior outside of the classroom must be in writing, and all teachers need to learn the procedures. One procedure could mandate a faculty member to escort any student discovered in serious conflict on the grounds to intensive care. This is much easier if the procedure is written as the school consequence for that behavior outside of the classroom. Upon infraction of school standards or guidelines, intensive care serves as a major consequence if a student becomes hostile or refuses direction from a faculty member or any adult in the school. The adult may escort the student to the homeroom teacher first or directly to ICU. A student to be placed in ICU is accompanied by either an adult assisting in the ICU or a school administrator. Afterwards, in most situations, the offended adult and the homeroom teacher meet with the DRC to discuss the best action to take with this student. Parents are often scheduled to meet with the DRC, teachers, and the student within 48 hours of the offense—and sooner if the behavior repeats.

With appropriate developmental-level adjustments, most consequences enforced in one grade usually work for another one. While making these minor adjustments, the student should always have a clear understanding of *why* the consequence is assigned. If a student can easily explain the reasoning in adequate detail and relate the offense to the consequence, then adjustments are developmentally appropriate. If uncertain about the appropriateness of the consequence, the teacher can simply ask the student to check the level of understanding. If there is any confusion, the teacher can apply another consequence. To increase effectiveness, grade-level teams can establish a pool of developmentally appropriate consequences. Along with this, clearly defined guidelines and additional procedures for teacher and student routines—from the beginning of the day until dismissal time—will reduce or eliminate these problems.

Using Routines to Clarify Expectations

Classroom expectations need to become routine: storing outdoor clothing; submitting homework assignments; returning notes (excuses for absence, transportation changes, work signed by parents, permission forms); trips to the school store, restroom, office, and cafeteria; morning work assignments; and sharpening pencils. Teachers can help clarify a routine's expectations and related responsibilities in class discussions, with role playing, and by posting checklists. Successful RCM teachers regularly review these expectations and engage students in additional role playing during the year, before the need arises.

Procedures for activities that bring structure to the day and provide increased opportunity for maximum engagement in learning should be established as part of RCM. Teachers can clarify these activities with written guidelines for students. Older students, as a class, may brainstorm a list of distractions, develop preventive procedures, and discuss natural and logical consequences for infractions. Using the pencil sharpener, individual trips to the restroom, discarding trash, illness during instruction, spontaneous thoughts students want to share with the teacher, and needing a Kleenex exemplify items that would occur on the initial list of distractions.

Most teachers attest that even students who are "perfect mon-sters" for one teacher are often at least civil and responsive to another. Through thoughtfully designed classroom-management strategies, teachers encourage responsible behavior by the same students in all settings. Both the teacher and the students know at all times what the teacher expects the students to do.

Dealing With Disruptive Classroom Behavior

How do the majority of students in the classroom feel when the other students' behaviors interfere with the right to a safe, orderly, and inviting learning environment? Teachers can engage students in discussions and role-playing activities to address these reactions. A consequence for disruptive behaviors during instruc-tion, for instance, might be that the violating student sits at a table or desk at the rear of the classroom during part of the class. A sign-in sheet at that spot documenting how the disruptive behav-ior prevented the student from participating in the usual manner could build internal control for the student.

Clear procedures that define expectations for students' responsi-ble behavior eliminate many potential problems. Each time a teacher interacts with an individual student or group during the school day, he can influence behavior. Words and actions determine whether the influence is positive or negative. Emotional tone conveys whether or not students are worthy of respect and able to experience success. To affirm students' ability to act responsibly, teachers must first establish an expectation that the students will act responsibly. The teacher's consistent response to unacceptable behavior—through enforcing natural or logical consequences—reinforces the expectation. Teachers, then, should persist in determining the right consequence for each individual student. When these consequences are exacer-bated, teachers can implement the ICU procedure.

CONSEQUENCES FOR MORE SERIOUS INFRACTIONS: THE INTENSIVE CARE UNIT (ICU)

In the hospital, when patients require more than routine nursing care, they may go to intensive care for closer monitoring. Educators can practice a similar procedure for the students who do not respond appropriately to preliminary consequences prescribed within the classroom. No longer should a teacher tolerate misbehavior that a student elects not to correct.

The Role of the DRC With RCM Design and ICU Management

The discipline review committee (DRC) leads the design of the school standards and guidelines, as discussed in Chapter 1. The DRC thus develops, monitors, and evaluates the school's RCMPlan™. This team should have no more than eight members, and include classroom and special area teachers. After electing a chairperson, the team leads the faculty in developing the school standards and guidelines, and then reviews and approves the plan for each grade level and for the school. This process upholds consistency in developing the schoolwide plan.

Once all of the standards, guidelines, and consequences are developed, the DRC establishes guidelines and procedures for the ICU. First, the DRC works with the school principal to find a location. Next, the DRC determines the procedures for supervising all ICU functions. As explained in Chapter 1, there should always be two individuals staffing the ICU—one to supervise and one to escort students from the classroom when called. In fact, many schools hire a full-time ICU coordinator to supervise the unit.

When considering behavior violations that warrant the ICU, two major types of behaviors prevail: type-A behaviors and type-B behaviors. Type-A behaviors relate to very serious infractions such as drugs, guns, fighting, and gang involvement—where federal, state and local laws, including school board policies, apply. RCM is not designed to treat these types of offenses, and these behavior problems should be immediately brought to the principal's attention. Type-B behaviors are behavioral in nature and violate standards and guidelines, such as not following the teacher's directions or arriving unprepared for class. These behaviors specifically fit The RCMPlan™.

Intensive care works only when a principal or an administrative team highly supports it. However, the RCMPlan™ seldom involves a member of the administrative team until level I contracts have been broken. Note: Some principals get involved when they really should not, but the principal or assistant principal is usually involved in the behavioral improvement (level II contracts). The RCMPlan™, again, allows principals to stay removed from common classroom and school discipline problems, designating teachers to handle a problem at the classroom level—where it should be handled. With RCM and through logical consequences, teachers no longer need to send students to the office for common classroom problems. If a student exhibits extremely disruptive misbehavior or shows intentional disrespect to the teacher, ICU provides the teacher with an added tool.

Planning Ahead for ICU

To maximize the success of The RCMPlan™, all available components or tools should be available before putting the plan into action. The steps taken by the DRC for establishing the ICU include:

1. Before school starts, establish a setting and tone for the ICU. The ideal environment for intensive care is a small classroom or mobile unit equipped with a selection of chairs of various sizes to accommodate students of different ages. The room should be a safe, supervised area.

2. Develop paperwork for ICU tracking, documentation, and parent reporting.

3. With the help of the administrative team, develop a schedule for supervision enlisting coverage from teacher assistants, administrative assistants, teachers, counselors, and office clerks. Usually, individuals are scheduled according to class periods for a week or two, but this varies greatly among schools. Some middle and high schools use classroom teachers. In most instances, each teacher serves only one to two weeks per year.

Two adults, in shifts of forty-five to ninety minutes, monitor the ICU, from school opening until the end of the school day. The monitors perform two functions: (1) supervising and recording student responses to what happened when the student first arrived and (2) recording any additional comments or negative behavior.

USING ICU EFFECTIVELY

A fictional student, Alex, will demonstrate how the ICU approach works. Alex is presently in Mrs. Smith's seventh grade class. Apparently, Alex had a difficult morning before coming to school. Mrs. Smith has already given him one consequence for breaking a guideline. During lunch, another teacher on lunch duty sees Alex throw food and subsequently takes him back to Mrs. Smith, who is teaching another class. Since the present environment is not effective for Alex at this time, this teacher, independently of Mrs. Smith, decides to send Alex to the intensive care unit. (If this is permitted according to the processes defined in the teacher handbook, if not, the teacher will follow the respective procedure, which may mean quietly interrupting Mrs. Smith.) Because the school's RCM procedure permits the teacher's independent use of ICU, she can quietly and without emotional display take Alex to intensive care, or call for assistance. The motive is not to embarrass Alex or to confront him at this time about his behavior. The motive is to address the inappropriate behavior with the least possible disruption to instruction.

If the event had occurred in Mrs. Smith class, or if the teacher who witnessed the offense had brought the student to her, Mrs. Smith could still have sent Alex to ICU. In this case, Mrs. Smith informs the office, and the office notifies the intensive care monitor. The monitor comes to the classroom and directs Alex to ICU. (Various systems can notify intensive care that a student needs admission—telephoning the ICU, notifying the main office for ICU assistance, or sending a trusted student to signal the need for ICU.)

When Alex enters intensive care, the supervisor immediately assigns him a seat and directs him to sit quietly until a monitor can talk with him. Once available, the monitor sits down with Alex and simply asks what has happened during the past thirty minutes. If Alex elects to talk, the monitor listens, making no comment and displaying no judgment either verbally or nonverbally. Alex can also choose not to talk, and sit quietly until Mrs. Smith is able to come to intensive care to talk to him.

In ICU, it is more effective if students are not assigned work. The goal is to help the student refocus, and receive guidance and direction from the teacher before returning to class. During ICU, students are directed to sit quietly, avoid talking, and resist sleeping. Along with allowing students to refocus and receive guidance, the ICU atmosphere itself is a deterrent. Most schools keep the room bare with nothing but chairs and a clock or two. In interviews about ICU with students of all ages, students relayed that they prefer to be in the classroom, behaving and completing their assignments, over sitting in ICU with no form of stimulation. Taking students' time is a powerful tool—word also gets around quickly about the boredom of the ICU. Most students will never return for a second visit.

Following the initial admittance, Mrs. Smith meets with Alex in the hall outside of the ICU at her earliest convenience. Like all teachers, Mrs. Smith has a "buddy-system plan" to summon assistance for class coverage—a teacher who has a planning period or a teacher who can see into the classroom and monitor behavior. Once there, Mrs. Smith sits down with Alex and resolves the issue in a caring, but firm, manner. Usually, the teacher asks questions to ascertain if the student is aware of the offending behavior that warranted ICU.

The questions sometimes focus on a pattern of behavior; consequences have been assigned, but not effective. In some cases, the student has been so disruptive in class that the teacher chooses ICU based on the severity of the disruption. In Alex's case, Mrs. Smith asks what happened, from his perception, and then asks him to reframe what he should have done.

Once Alex convinces Mrs. Smith that he has resolved the problem, and his behavior is under control, he returns to the classroom. Mrs. Smith then completes a form that describes the inappropriate behaviors, explains the expected responsible behavior, and details how the situation was resolved. This form should remain simple but provide adequate information. The ICU monitor receives a copy of the document to file in the office and another is mailed to the parent. If Alex refuses to correct his behavior or talks and acts out during intensive care, he remains there until the principal or assistant principal can intervene. Generally, violating the behavior requirements in ICU results in the student being taken to the office and the principal most likely suspends the student.

FAQs: The ICU

Q: How long should a classroom behavior be tolerated before the misbehaving student is placed in intensive care?

A: In the above scenario, Alex may have been having problems for two or three days before he was sent to intensive care, or his inappropriate behavior may have occurred two minutes before he was removed from the room. A formula is hard to use. The maxim to remember is that no student has the right to interfere with the learning of another. We recommend ICU when a student has been disrupting instruction and no other consequence is working, or when there is intentional disrespect to a teacher or adult working in the school.

Q: What is the recommended maximum length of a stay in intensive care?

A: There are no time limits for stays in intensive care. The teacher— a professional capable of making responsible decisions— determines the length of time a student remains. Hopefully, the teacher's professional judgment and care for the student will weigh heavily in determining an effective length of stay. Most middle or secondary students remain no more than twenty minutes.

Q: Should a student be expected to complete work missed while in ICU?

A: No, we have found that students are not actively engaged before they are sent to ICU and it is better for students to reflect upon what they have done. The boredom of the room, the extra quiet time, and the interview with the teacher are most effective. Most students do not return if the ICU visit is conducted properly. Parents may not understand this rationale at first, yet it can be explained. For example, one superintendent received a call about a student not having any work to do in ICU, and he simply responded that there was plenty of work for this student to do in his classroom. Once he is permitted to return to class, the superintendent explained, he could avoid this problem by not breaking any guidelines.

Monitoring the ICU

Teachers or teacher assistants usually serve as ICU supervisors on a rotational basis. Most middle and high school students have more than two or three teachers, and when the student is sent to ICU, the supervisory teacher or ICU director writes up the short form and sends documents to the relevant individuals (DRC chair, principal, parents, and the student). After a student is sent to ICU a second time, the DRC guides and monitors the process and meets with the student, the parents, and all of the teachers involved; they next develop a plan or approach to avoid the last and final trip to ICU.

BEHAVIOR IMPROVEMENT AGREEMENTS (BIAs)

In the very unlikely event that ICU does not work after the third visit, the next consequence assigned by the DRC is the **behavior improvement agreement (BIA)**. There are two levels—a BIA I and a BIA II. When the DRC uses the BIA I, the chairperson informs the student and parents that all other attempted approaches to correct the undesirable behavior have been unsuccessful. The student, a parent or guardian, and all teachers involved with the student then meet to develop the BIA I. This plan differs from the social and academic contracts used for groups or individuals to reward achievement or manage instruction. The agreement approach in The RCMPlan™ is the final attempt to improve behavior before the principal and DRC mandate major corrective action in the form of BIA II.

BIA I

For BIA I, the teacher prepares a list of improper behaviors that must be discontinued, and together with the DRC, finalizes the plan. After the meeting with parents and the student, the student signs the agreement (parents can also sign) and both the parents and the student receive a copy. The DRC keeps the original and a copy of the agreement is also kept in a designated file in the school office. If no agreement is reached in the meeting, the principal is notified and takes over the case. The DRC is then relieved of all future responsibilities with this student.

All DRC and BIA forms can be downloaded and personalized with school name from the DRC/BIA link on The RCMPlan™ Web site, www.rcmplan.com.

BIA II

A BIA II is used in cases when intensive care is not effective and the BIA I is broken. First, the DRC enforces the consequences for breaking BIA I. This may be school suspension, if approved by the principal, or some other major consequence. While formulas are not the best approach, the DRC meets again with the parents and all involved teachers; this time, the principal joins the meeting and assists in developing of the BIA II.

To initiate this process, the school principal or an assistant principal meets with the DRC to develop the BIA II, which is, again, the school's final attempt to handle the student and the problem. Regardless of when it is used, the agreement has the same three components as BIA I—promised behaviors, consequences, and the signatures of the involved parties.

In designing an agreement, the DRC and the principal usually develop one major consequence that is much stronger than in the first agreement, usually long-term suspension, expulsion, or available assistance from the juvenile justice system. At the meeting, the student, parent, and DRC chairperson sign the agreement with copies, once again duplicated for the student, parents, and appropriate teachers. This time, the principal keeps the original. If the agreement is broken, the principal takes necessary action to administer the stated consequence. Level II BIAs should occur with only the most difficult students—less than 2 percent of students in the middle or secondary school. With this approach, the student learns, for example, that if she is suspended, it is a result of her action and not the principal's.

THE DRC'S SUPERVISORY PROCESS

Faculty and staff develop The RCMPlan™ under the direction and supervision of the DRC; the plan should contain the overall school standard and school guidelines, as recommended by the faculty and student representatives. After each set of guidelines, such as guidelines for hall behavior, parking lot, cafeteria, and other locations, a *specific* consequence is described. Procedures for staff to follow in working with infractions by students should be included. The DRC then presents the school plan to the administration, faculty, and staff for adoption or modification.

In the next step, individual teachers at the various grade levels and special areas establish classroom guidelines based upon school standards (or use the three we suggest) and a pool of logical consequences for classroom use. After the first year, the faculty might seek student input as appropriate for revisions. This input allows students to be more involved in decision making and models participatory citizenship. Teachers, however, should oversee consequences. The DRC then receives the revised plans for review (see samples on the Web site).

After the classroom plans are added to the school plan, the administration and staff establish the ICU. Once underway, the DRC monitors how effectively teachers use it. The DRC also assists teachers who need more guidance in ICU procedures and they report any intentional abuse of ICU to the principal.

Prior to the implementation of The RCMPlan™, the principal, or a highly respected staff member, notifies students, by grade level, about RCM procedures. The final stage entails notifying parents of the plan by letter and at open house—both preferably before school begins.

Once the DRC finalizes school standards, guidelines, and consequences, the committee writes a plan for working with extremely difficult students. The following ten steps outline this process:

1. Broken standards or guidelines.

   Type-A Behaviors: Legal/Laws Broken

   Student goes to the principal because a federal, state, or local law is broken. This also includes violations of school board policies.

Type-B Behaviors: Inappropriate Behaviors

Student receives a consequence. Consequences should not be limited to a certain number before becoming an ICU offense. It varies according to the tolerance level of the teacher or the level of the offense. For example, a student may receive five consequences before being sent to ICU. In another situation, the behavior is so severe that ICU is the first consequence. We strongly recommend a vast number of consequences before ICU. The ICU equates to sending the student to the office in other or older models.

2. ICU procedures.

First Offense

ICU personnel calls parent.

Second Offense

DRC conducts a parent conference. Sometimes, parties attending the conference write a plan for improvement to help the student work with teachers and parents, and to hopefully avoid a third and final ICU offense.

3. BIA I development.

Upon a third offense, the ICU coordinator or supervisor contacts the individuals who placed the student in ICU each of the three times, and also informs the DRC chairperson. Parties meet to write up a BIA I for the student. Once the BIA I is completed, the DRC sets up a meeting with the parents, teachers, and the student. After the meeting and once all signatures are completed, the involved teachers, the student, parents, and office receive copies of the BIA I.

4. Post-ICU third offense.

BIA I students *never* return to ICU for any reason. After the third visit, research clearly indicates that the ICU does not work for this type of student. Instead, the student meets weekly or monthly with the DRC or a faculty mentor, as assigned. The DRC can modify or void the contract at any time for excellent improvement over a period of six months or more.

5. BIA I infraction.

The student is assigned to the DRC chairperson or a school administrator.

6. BIA II development.

A member of the DRC, the witness (adult) to the BIA I infraction, and the principal meet to design the BIA II.

7. Principal monitoring.

Once the BIA II is developed, the principal meets with the student on a regularly scheduled basis. With noted improvement, the principal may refer the student back to the DRC for reconsideration.

8. BIA II infraction.

If the BIA II is broken, the principal assigns the consequence. In most cases, the student is immediately suspended based upon state law and board policy.

9. Return to school.

When the student returns to school, the student may follow an alternative or reduced schedule (as determined by the principal) and attend daily group/individual counseling sessions or be referred to an appropriate juvenile justice personnel. If assigned to a counselor, the principal receives regular updates on the progress, without any confidentiality violations between the counselor and the student. The counselor can also recommend outside assistance within the laws of the state.

10. Final alternatives to failed BIAs.

If behavior does not improve with counseling or initial attempts with outside assistance, the DRC, counselor, central-office personnel, legal advisor, and principal meet to recommend the next step. This may include options such as alternative classes, evening school, alternative school, juvenile court, or expulsion.

A SAMPLE OF GRADE-SPECIFIC CONSEQUENCES

Here are some suggested consequences for sixth grade students, aligned to sample classroom standards, guidelines, and expected behaviors. Additional consequences appear in The RCMPlan™ Toolbox in Resource B.

Standard: I am responsible for my actions.

Guideline 1: The student will come to school prepared and ready to learn.

Expected Behavior 1: The student will be prepared for class with needed materials such as pencils, pens, paper, books, PE clothes, or other requested items.

Suggested consequences:

- Student receives verbal reminder.
- Student rents or trades something for needed materials.
- Teacher mails a written note home.
- Teacher develops agreement with student and parent.
- Teacher implements a daily contact sheet with parent.
- Teacher has telephone conference with parent.
- Teacher has parent conference at school.
- Student has counselor conference.
- DRC representative has parent conference.

Expected Behavior 2: The student will not be in possession of cell phones, beepers, pagers, lighters, headphones, CDs, or other multimedia devices.

Suggested Consequences:

- Teacher or attending adult confiscate item, allowing parents to retrieve.
- Item is returned at the end of the term.
- Item is not returned.

Expected Behavior 3: The student will dress appropriately. The student will follow the dress code.

Suggested Consequences:

- Student receives verbal recognition.
- Student changes into appropriate apparel.
- Teacher has conference with student.
- Student is sent home to change clothes.

Expected Behavior 4: The student will not wear hats or caps in the building.

Suggested Consequences:

- Student receives verbal warning.
- Teacher or attending adult confiscates item, and allows parents to retrieve.
- Item is not returned.

Expected Behavior 5: The student will not have food or drink outside the cafeteria, with the exception of bottled water.

Suggested Consequences:

- Student receives verbal reminder.
- Teacher or attending adult confiscate item and item is returned later.
- Teacher or attending adult confiscate item and it is not returned.
- Student receives written disciplinary statement.
- Teacher has telephone conference with parent.
- Teacher has conference with parent at school.
- Student has counselor conference.

Expected Behavior 6: The student will be in possession of needed hearing aids, glasses, and other necessary devices.

Suggested Consequences:

- Student receives verbal recognition.
- Teacher or attending adult verbally redirects student.

- Teacher has counselor conference.
- Teacher develops contract with student and parent.

Expected Behavior 7: The student will attend all scheduled classes.

Suggested Consequences:

- Teacher has telephone conference with parent.
- Student loses privileges for extracurricular activity.
- Student writes responsibility statement.
- Student receives afterschool detention.
- Teacher develops contract with student and parent.
- Teacher assigns related chores/work detail.
- Parent shadows student at school.
- Student is escorted to and from class.
- Student attends Saturday school.

Expected Behavior 8: The student will actively participate in class, exhibit a positive attitude, and display attentive behavior.

Suggested Consequences:

- Teacher verbally redirects student.
- Student receives verbal warning.
- Student writes responsibility statement.
- Teacher refers student to counselor.
- Teacher changes instructional approach.
- Teacher has telephone conference with parent.
- Teacher has parent conference at school.
- Teacher implements daily contact sheet with parent.
- Teacher designs behavior-checkpoint system to better guide the student.

Expected Behavior 9: The student will not disturb the learning of others.

Suggested Consequences:
- Teacher verbally redirects student.
- Student receives verbal warning.

- Student writes responsibility statement.
- Teacher mails written note home.
- Student has counselor conference.
- Class meets with discipline committee/class court.
- Teacher has parent conference at school.
- DRC representative has conference with student.
- Teacher, student, parent, and counselor have conference.
- Teacher initiates daily contact sheet with parent.
- Teacher designs behavior-checkpoint system to better guide the student.
- Teacher and student develop individualized behavior contract.
- Student loses privileges for extracurricular activity.
- Student receives schedule change.
- Student is assigned to ICU.

Expected Behavior 10: The student will not sleep in class.

Suggested Consequences:

- Student receives verbal warning.
- Teacher mails written note home.
- Student attends counseling.
- Teacher has telephone conference with parent.
- Teacher has parent conference at school.
- Teacher initiates daily communications with parent.

The RCMPlan™ Toolbox in Resource B contains numerous examples of consequences and related guidelines. Schools can also visit follow the "Consequences" link on the Web site. (Click on "Consequences," find the appropriate grade level and specific behavior, and download numerous consequences for use in school or an individual classroom.) While consequences are intended and encouraged for anyone using RCM, those that teachers develop in teams or with the school faculty are most common and effective.

GROUP ACTIVITIES

1. Rate the following misbehavior problems by priority and then try to come to a consensus. To what degree do the

agreed behaviors occur in your classroom and to what degree (how severe) do you usually experience them?

____Incomplete Homework

____Call Outs

____Minor Classroom Disruptions (e.g., two students whispering and off-task)

____Major Classroom Disruptions (e.g., continuous talking, interruptions, abrupt behavior)

____Disrespect to Classmates

____Disrespect to the Teacher

____Unintentional Profanity (slips out and not focused on anyone)

____Intentional Profanity to Another Student

____Intentional Profanity to the Teacher

____Forgetting Supplies

____Other Behaviors the Group May Develop

2. Categorize the behaviors and work in pairs or triads to come up with at least three different logical consequences that could be used with each specific behavior.

3. Repeat the activity above for out-of-classroom behaviors such as lunchroom or hallways.

4. Discuss the top three inappropriate behaviors that would rate as ICU offenses.

5. Repeat the activity above for out-of-classroom ICU offenses.

6. As individual teachers, how do you feel about taking turns assisting as a supervisor two or three times a year (maybe two or three weeks in smaller schools)? List concern and suggestions.

LOOKING AHEAD

This chapter presented the use of logical consequences and how they fit into The RCMPlan™, highlighting the DRC's role, particularly in respect to the development and implementation of the ICU. The chapter also covered the two behavioral improvement agreements, with several samples. Next, Resource A includes The RCMPlan™ Principal's Guide, followed by The RCMPlan™ Toolbox in Resource B. The Principal's Guide lists the steps and codes the readings, tools, and Web site resources necessary for full implementation of The RCMPlan™.

Resource A

The RCMPlan™ Principal's Guide

Pilot programs of The RCMPlan™ in hundreds of schools show that, by far, the support of school leaders is the greatest contributor to RCM's success. The skill of the principal, or other facilitator, in introducing, implementing, and monitoring this schoolwide discipline plan is essential in this leadership. This principal's guide shows, at a glance, how to successfully implement and monitor The RCMPlan™ by identifying:

- each step of the process
- the purpose of each step
- the participants
- the time required to implement each step
- the tools and materials needed for each step

Step # With Time Requirements	Participants	Related Book Chapters	The RCMPlan™ Toolbox	The RCMPlan™ Web site (www.rcmplan.com)
Step 1: select and prepare the discipline review committee (DRC) for faculty and staff development. Time: varies for reading the entire book. Time: 3 to 4 days for staff development for DRC.	Principal and DRC members: the principal selects DRC members and leads a book study to prepare everyone for their various roles in implementing and sustaining The RCMPlan™.	Entire book.	Tool #1: Selecting and Preparing the Discipline Review Committee.	Link: The DRC. Select "Preparing the DRC;" choose methods 1 to 4: 1. PowerPoint. 2. Narrated DVD with school visit. 3. DRC seminars. 4. On-site trainer.
Step 2: develop the school standard(s) and guidelines. Time: varies for reading the Introduction, Chapter 1, and Chapter 2. Time: 1 to 1½ days for faculty and staff development.	Total faculty and staff: the principal and the DRC lead the faculty and staff in developing the school's standard (s) and guidelines.	Introduction, Chapter 1, and Chapter 2.	Tool #2: Developing the School Standard(s) and Guidelines. Tool #3: Sample Middle or High School Model for School Standards and Guidelines.	Link: The School Standards and Guidelines. Select "Middle or High School;" choose methods 1 to 4: 1. Narrated PowerPoint. 2. Middle school samples (Word and PDF files). 3. High school samples (Word and PDF files). 4. On-site trainer.

Step # With Time Requirements	Participants	Related Book Chapters	The RCMPlan™ Toolbox	The RCMPlan™ Web site (www.rcmplan.com)
Step 3: develop grade-level standards, guidelines, and expected behaviors. Time: varies for reviewing and reading chapters. Time: ½ day to 1 day for faculty and staff development.	Middle or senior high subject or grade-level teams: the DRC leads the teams in developing the subject or grade-level standard(s), guidelines, and expected behaviors.	Introduction, Chapter 1, and Chapter 2.	Tool #4: Developing the Grade-Level Standards, Guidelines and Expected Behaviors. Tool #5: Sample Middle or High School Model for Grade-Level Standards, Guidelines, and Expected Behaviors.	Link: Grade or Subject- Level Teams, Standards, Guidelines, and Expected Behaviors. Select "Middle or High School;" choose methods 1 to 3: 1. Middle school samples (Word and PDF files). 2. High school samples (Word and PDF files). 3. On-site trainer.
Step 4: develop school consequences for specific school guidelines. Time: varies for reading. Time: ½ day for faculty and staff development.	Total faculty and staff: the principal and DRC lead the faculty and staff in developing the school consequences for violating specific guidelines.	Chapter 4, "Using Logical Consequences Versus Punishment."	Tool #6: Developing the School Consequences. Tool #7: Sample Middle or High School Model for School Consequences.	Link: School and Grade, Subject, Team Consequences. Select "Middle or High School;" choose methods 1 to 3: 1. Middle school samples (Word and PDF files). 2. High school samples (Word and PDF files). 3. On-site trainer.

(Continued)

(Continued)

Step # With Time Requirements	Participants	Related Book Chapters	The RCMPlan™ Toolbox	The RCMPlan™ Web site (www.rcmplan.com)
Step 5: develop grade-level consequences for expected behaviors. Time: varies for reading. Time: ½ day for faculty and staff development.	Subject or grade-level teams: the DRC leads the teams in developing a pool of consequences for violating grade-level expected behaviors.	Chapter 4, "Developing a Pool of Consequences for Selective Use in the Classroom."	Tool #8: Developing Grade-Level Consequences. Tool #9: Sample Middle or High School Model for Grade-Level Consequences.	Link: School and Grade, Subject, Team Consequences. Select "Middle School Open Middle Grades;" choose methods 1 to 4: 1. Narrated PowerPoint. 2. Individual subject and grade-level samples 6–8 (Word and PDF files). Link: School and Grade, Subject, Team Consequences. Select "High School Open High School Subjects and Grades;" choose methods 1 to 4: 1. Narrated PowerPoint. 2. Individual subject and grade-level samples 9–12 (Word and PDF files). 3. Book of 101 Consequences for Grades 6–12. 4. On-site trainer.

Step # With Time Requirements	Participants	Related Book Chapters	The RCMPlan™ Toolbox	The RCMPlan™ Web site (www.rcmplan.com)
Step 6: implement the ICU, BIA I, and BIA II. Time: varies for reading. Time: 1 to 1½ days.	Total faculty: the DRC instructs the faculty and staff in developing the structure, function, and procedures for the ICU and BIAs.	Chapter 4, ICU and BIA sections.	Tool #10: Using the ICU, BIA I, and BIA II in the Middle or High School. Tool #11: Sample Middle or High School Model for ICU and BIA Procedures.	Link: ICU and BIAs. Select "Middle School;" choose methods 1 to 4: 1. Narrated PowerPoint. 2. Using the ICU, BIA I, and BIA II (Word and PDF files). 3. DRC and BIA forms for downloading. 4. On-site trainer. Link: ICU and BIAs. Select "High School;" choose methods 1 to 4: 1. Narrated PowerPoint. 2. Using the ICU, BIA I, and BIA II (Word and PDF files). 3. DRC and BIA forms for downloading. 4. On-site trainer.
Step 7: teach responsibility to students in an inviting environment. Time: varies for reading. Time: 1 to 1½ days.	Subject or grade-level teams: the DRC leads the teams in developing lesson plans for teaching	Chapter 2.	Tool #12: Teaching Responsibility in an Inviting Environment.	Link: Teaching Responsibility. Select "Middle School;" choose methods 1 to 4: 1. DVD: *The Art and Science of Teaching Responsibility to Students.*

(Continued)

Step # With Time Requirements	Participants	Related Book Chapters	The RCMPlan™ Toolbox	The RCMPlan™ Web site (www.rcmplan.com)
	responsibility in a warm and inviting environment.			2. Staff development scenarios for teaching responsibility and civility (Word and PDF files). 3. Teacher workbook: *The Inviting Classroom for Developing Student Responsibility.* 4. On-site trainer.
Step 8: finalize preparations for the first school day. Time: varies for reading. Time: 1 to 1½ days.	Total faculty and staff.	Complete book for resources.	Tool #13: The RCMPlan™ Checklist. Tool #14: Finalizing The RCMPlan™: Bringing It All Together.	Link: Teaching Responsibility. Select "High School;" choose methods 1 to 4: 1. DVD: *The Art and Science of Teaching Responsibility to Students.* 2. Staff development scenarios for teaching responsibility and civility (Word and PDF files). 3. Teacher workbook: *The Inviting Classroom for Developing Student Responsibility.* 4. On-site trainer. Link: The RCMPlan™ Teacher Handbook. Select "Middle School or High School" Link: The First Day of School Checklist. Select "Middle or High School."

Resource B

The RCMPlan™ Toolbox

Tool #1: Selecting and Preparing the Discipline Review Committee

1. Establish the DRC with no less than five or more than eleven individuals to represent each grade level or subject area. The best size is five to seven members.

2. Include individuals to represent special area teachers and special education teachers. Try to balance the committee by race and gender. Equal representation is important in all areas.

3. Consider putting a teacher assistant, if available, on the committee.

4. Do not put an assistant principal or principal assistant on the DRC, as this is a faculty committee.

5. Allow the DRC to select the chairperson, unless there is a special circumstance.

Who should be on the DRC? In many situations, schools already have a discipline committee or a school improvement team (SIT). Some principals choose this same group as the DRC if they think these individuals can assume the tasks of DRC members. Some teachers volunteer for the DRC, but this is rare. Usually, the principal appoints the DRC for the first two years. For the third year, the faculty can elect the DRC members.

Criteria and characteristics for being on the DRC should include:

- teachers who have a week during the school year to devote to training with the principal and one or two afternoons after school during the school year, with or without compensation
- respected individuals who are considered good teachers by their peers
- individuals who are strong enough emotionally to confront teachers not effectively practicing RCM in their classrooms
- individuals who are very open to change and improvement

One of the best ways to motivate teachers to volunteer or nominate their peers is to make sure faculty understand the above points.

In some situations, a teacher or a group of teachers have heard about an RCM school or have worked in one; this can help the principal accomplish two things: (1) securing DRC members and (2) motivating other teacher(s) to want The RCMPlan™ implementation.

One principal described it this way:

I became the principal of a new school twenty years ago; I was a fan of the effective schools movement and what was known as the related findings, the "correlates of effective schools." One of those correlates identified was "safe and orderly schools." The effective schools research strongly correlated statistically with high student achievement and active engagement. This resulted in higher time on tasks for improved achievement and the development of strong schoolwide discipline programs, with related, effective classroom-management practices used by teachers.

Being aware of the research and the need for the implementation of safe and orderly schools, I assembled a new school staff meeting a few days before the students arrived, and the issue of a designing a schoolwide discipline plan rose to the forefront of importance—it actually dominated the agenda during the meeting. The school-improvement team was composed of teachers who had previously taught at seven different schools. They shared several different perspectives of the major design and related components embedded in the most effective schoolwide discipline plan actually needed for the new school. In opening a new school, the faculty, staff and administrative team had the luxury of starting with a blank slate.

During the continued discussion, one of the teachers described a schoolwide discipline and classroom management program being used in a school in a neighboring district (one that had started the school year a week prior), referred to as "responsible classroom management." A fellow teacher from the neighboring school had been raving about the high rate of success and the almost overnight improvement the faculty had discovered with the implementation, of what was briefly referred to as RCM. Enthusiasm of the teacher's description was pleasantly contagious to the rest of the group and I was asked to contact the RCM school principal to arrange a visit for seven of these highly motivated teachers and what was to become, the following week, our discipline review committee preparing to implement RCM. (J. R. Watson, former principal and district superintendent, personal communication, October 7, 2009)

This former principal had one of the most effective RCM schools, and for many years, supported The RCMPlan™ in schools districtwide.

Many schools principals, then, hear about The RCMPlan™ from a teacher, who heard from another teacher. The principal subsequently wants to visit the school. In a nutshell, real success can begin when the principal, or a respected faculty member, hears about RCM; or, perhaps the easiest way, individuals or groups of teachers can read this book. In any case, an effective principal who knows the faculty, staff, and students will find the best way to support the program.

PREPARING THE DISCIPLINE REVIEW COMMITTEE

DRC members tend to learn fast and they strongly support the program. Highly motivated teachers make RCM implementation easier for the principal.

The principal should allow the DRC ample time to read about The RCMPlan™ and digest the content. In other models, teachers control most discipline and students have very little time to process the purpose of classroom discipline. Therefore, both teachers and students need time to adjust to a student-internalized discipline program.

The principal spends a week working directly with the faculty in two similar, but arguably different, areas: (1) gaining knowledge of all the content, concepts, and elements of The RCMPlan™—from learning the differences between standards and guidelines through the use of the DRC, BIA I, and BIA II; and (2) learning to use The RCMPlan™ Toolbox.

During the week with faculty, in preparing the DRC, the principal should combine school visits, presentations, and discussions of the PowerPoint and/or DVD from The RCMPlan™ Web site. In most schools, the principal and/or teacher trainers can effectively prepare the entire faculty for implementation of RCM with the book, Toolbox, and Web site materials. However, in the case of time constraints or space limitations, training seminars are available off campus for principals, teacher trainers, or the entire faculty. These sessions range from introducing RCM to full implementation of the program. Master trainers also conduct similar sessions on-site (from introduction to full implementation) for the individual school or district. (Please check the Web site for locations and dates of training seminars, and for details and availability of master trainers.)

EXAMPLE OF DRC PROCEDURES FROM THE FACULTY HANDBOOK

The discipline review committee assists the principal by ensuring that classroom discipline problems are corrected with the full implementation of RCM. The DRC also works closely with the ICU coordinator to maximize the effects of The RCMPlan™.

Committee Members

- DRC chair elected by the committee
- ninth grade representative for high school or sixth grade representative for middle school
- tenth grade representative for high school or seventh grade representative for middle school

- eleventh grade representative for high school or eighth grade representative for middle school
- twelfth grade representative for high school (some larger middle and high schools place two representatives from each grade)
- special education representative (individuals from each grade level)
- special/elective subject representative
- school counselor

Selection, Rotation, and Election of DRC Members

- The principal appoints grade-level representatives, special subject and special education representatives, and the school counselor to serve on the DRC committee for the initial year of implementation; the elected chair serves a two-year term.
- By the end of the month before school starts, the appointed DRC committee elects, by secret ballot, a chairperson and a cochair for the current school year.
- All appointed members, with the exception of the school counselor and the elected cochair, serve as members for one school year.
- The school counselor holds a continuing position on the DRC.
- The cochair serves a two-year term, assuming role of chairperson in the second year, which ensures consistency of goals and general responsibilities.
- Each grade level annually elects its own representative to serve on the DRC, as does the special education faculty. The DRC then elects a chair and cochair.
- The DRC completes elections by the end of the month before school ends in order to submit a DRC member list to the principal for the following school year.
- The DRC submits a proposed agenda for the following school year.
- The DRC begins each school year focused on needs identified by former members and members serving dual terms.

Responsibilities of the Discipline Review Committee

- Present the finalized RCM program to the faculty for review and approval.

- Create student guides and teacher manuals for the school.
- Serve as the RCM liaison between classroom teachers, students, parents, and the principal.
- Provide necessary training, offer support strategies for classroom discipline, and monitor ICU procedures.
- Encourage the faculty to share their concerns by discussing issues with the chairperson or cochair of the DRC.
- Encourage the faculty to voice their concerns in writing via the DRC mailbox.
- Monitor and evaluate RCM.
- Monitor the appropriate use of ICU.
- Develop and monitor BIA I.
- Develop and monitor BIA II.

Annual DRC Responsibilities

- Elect a DRC chairperson and cochair by the end of August.
- Review The RCMPlan™ components.
- Review procedures for ICU and BIAs to ensure effectiveness.
- Work with the principal and faculty to determine any additional expected behaviors outside the classroom—including the halls, cafeteria, and playground.
- Review and revise the RCM student guide and teacher manual.
- Elect new committee members and submit a proposed agenda for the following school year.

Meeting Times

- Meet weekly on selected afternoons beginning at an agreed time.

Final Review Prior to Implementation of RCM

- Identify any specific problems with the RCM procedures.
- Assign responsibility to the chairperson or cochair for communicating emergencies to all committee members via e-mail, memo, telephone conference, etc.
- Design procedures for dealing with ICU and BIA offenses.
- Publish a student guide to communicate components of RCM to students.
- Publish a teacher handbook to communicate components of RCM to teachers.

Tool #2: Developing the School Standard(s) and Guidelines

To achieve maximum success and efficiency in this step, the principal can download the narrated PowerPoint and reference other resources from the Web site. To further assist the faculty in developing the standard and guidelines for the school, the principal also must require the faculty and staff to read the both Introduction and Chapter 1, in detail, prior to any training sessions.

- The principal and faculty should reserve ample time to discuss whether one standard is adequate for the school. We strongly suggest the sole standard schoolwide, "I am responsible for all my actions."
- Once the DRC and principal approve one or more standards, they decide where and how to publish the standard(s) throughout the school, considering the lunchroom, restrooms, media center, locations visible when entering and exiting, and every classroom. Along with signage, many schools paint the maxims on the walls.
- The principal and DRC next determine specific guidelines for out-of-classroom behavior. These vary from three to seven guidelines, and usually include hallways, restrooms, media center, gym, and busses. Guidelines appear in similar areas as the standards, but with lighter emphasis. Once students are taught the actions of the guidelines, they are reinforced through instruction.
- The principal and DRC focus on the standard and guidelines, without exploring consequences as this stage. While school guidelines will have a fixed consequence, posted throughout the school and included within handbooks and school literature, consequences for grade-level standards and guidelines appear more selectively.

Tool #3: Sample Middle or High School Model for School Standard and Guidelines

SCHOOL STANDARDS, GUIDELINES, EXPECTED BEHAVIORS, AND CONSEQUENCES

School Standard

I am responsible for my actions.

School Guidelines

Guideline 1   Any serious or continuous act of student behavior that disrupts the educational process will not be tolerated.

Consequence   Observing adult takes the student to ICU, and ICU supervisor informs homeroom teacher.

Guideline 2   Profanity or obscene language is not allowed.

Consequence   Observing adult takes the student to ICU, and ICU supervisor informs homeroom teacher.

Guideline 3   Failure to respond to a reasonable request by an adult, or lying or cheating to deceive school authorities, will not be tolerated.

Consequence   Observing adult takes the student to ICU, and ICU supervisor informs homeroom teacher.

Guideline 4   Illegal or antisocial behaviors will not be tolerated. These classify as follows:

- Physically attacking or threatening to strike any school employee or any adult at school.
- Assaulting, attacking, or threatening to cause physical injury to a student by two or more students, and/or any assault resulting in serious personal injury by one or more student.
- Extorting or maliciously threatening another student to gain money or objects belonging to others.
- Possessing weapons.

- Arson, vandalism, unlawful entry, or theft.
- Selling, possessing, distributing, or being under the influence of alcohol, tobacco products, or other illegal drugs.
- Verbal threats, physical assaults, or intentional acts that clearly threaten the safety of others.
- Any act of a sexual nature.
- Directing obscene language and/or gestures toward any persons.
- Leaving class without teacher/principal permission.
- Breaking federal, state, or local laws.
- Violations of any school district behavior guideline.

Consequence   Observing adult immediately notifies principal to determine legal or other appropriate action.

Expected Behaviors/Procedures for Special Areas and Outside the Classroom

All teachers and adults at the middle or high school are responsible for establishing expected behaviors/procedures for special areas and school locations outside the classroom for students. All teachers and adults are expected to use these behaviors to guide students in their development toward becoming individuals responsible for their own actions. These behavior expectations are the same for sixth through twelfth graders.

Continuity and consistency are important for all students. The expected behaviors allow the responsible adults a mechanism for setting the direction and for guiding students in safe, responsible behavior. The DRC, principal, and faculty finalize the following behaviors/procedures for students.

Cafeteria Behaviors

All students will:

- Walk at all times.
- Move quickly through the lunch line.
- Have lunch money or numbers ready for the cashier.

- Talk in a normal voice and not shout at people at other tables.
- Not take other people's food, trade food, or share food.
- Not throw food, play with food, or use food in any creative way.
- Use good table manners including saying please and thank you, chewing with mouths closed, using utensils, and keeping conversation to appropriate topics.
- Keep trash and food off the tables and floors.
- Dispose of trash in the receptacles in an environmental, safe way.
- Return trays to the cleaning window.
- Stay seated until dismissed by the teacher or adult.

Restroom Behaviors

All students will:

- Use the restroom silently.
- Use the restroom with no more than three other students.
- Flush the toilet after use.
- Wash hands and dispose of paper towels in the trashcan.
- Turn off the water after use.
- Respect the privacy of others in the stalls.

Hallway Behaviors

All students will:

- Walk at all times.
- Walk on the right-hand side of the hallway.
- Keep hands and feet to themselves.
- Keep trash off the floors.

Bus Behaviors

All students will:

- Be respectful, listen to, and follow a bus driver's request, promptly and politely.
- Ride to and from school using assigned busses or routes. If there is a need to ride another bus, students must have written permission from parents or guardian.

- Remain seated in the forward position.
- Keep the aisles free from hands, feet, and objects.
- Not litter on the bus.
- Not eat, drink, or chew on the bus.
- Not throw any object on, at, or out of the bus.
- Wait until the bus has come to a full stop before getting off the bus.
- Get off the bus at assigned bus stop and always cross in front of the bus, if necessary.
- Remain silent while the bus is stopped at a railroad crossing.

Car-Ride Behaviors

All students will:

- Report promptly to the pick-up area and to the classroom from drop-off point.
- Be respectful, listen to, and follow car-duty supervisor's requests, promptly and politely.
- Watch for the arrival of car-duty supervisor's vehicle.
- Remain seated until all cars are at a complete stop.
- Not eat, drink, or chew in the car.
- Not throw any object at or out of a car.
- Talk in whisper-level voices.

Gym Behavior

All students will:

- Respect gym teacher or gym supervisors, other students, and the environment.
- Follow any specific behaviors established by the gym teacher.
- Remain in the gym until dismissed by the gym teacher.
- Use the bathroom before going outside.
- Ask permission to go inside if it is necessary.
- Wear appropriate clothing, including coats if directed.
- Use gym equipment appropriately (i.e., no jumping from high places or swings, no standing or walking on top of equipment, no pushing on equipment).

- Use respectful words when playing and solving problems (i.e., no name-calling, put downs, or inappropriate language).
- Collect and return all equipment to the gymnasium.

Media Center Behaviors

All students will:

- Use the Internet, software, and computer menus for responsible academic learning directly related to schoolwork.
- Respect the privacy of their own and other people's files.
- Not violate or attempt to violate the security system.
- Not interfere with system performance, access information not directly related to schoolwork, enter someone else's file (with or without permission), or use someone else's password.
- Not change any operating commands in the system.
- Not eat, drink, or chew around the computers.
- Report access to any inappropriate materials to an adult.

School Assembly/Performance Behaviors

All students will:

- Sit on bleachers or cross-legged on floor.
- Pay attention to the speaker or presenter.
- Applaud at appropriate times.
- Participate in activities.
- Talk only at appropriate times.
- Keep hands and feet to themselves.

Tool #4: Developing the Grade-Level Standards, Guidelines, and Expected Behaviors

The DRC members prepare the grade-level middle or high school teams.

- Team members must review the Introduction, Chapter 1, and Chapter 2 in detail prior to the seminar.
- The DRC conducts this training, usually beginning with the PowerPoint downloaded from the Web site.
- Usually after the introduction of student standards and guidelines, the teams decide whether to use the same standard and the three major guidelines schoolwide.
- The teams accept the suggested model or add additional guidelines—extra guidelines for the classroom should be implemented with caution, as these become more like rules. While permitted in the school model, where all faculty and staff monitor and ascribe to predetermined actions, the case is different in the classroom.
- After developing the guidelines, teams designate the expected behaviors according to developmental age levels, aligned by grades. Tool #5 models specific behavioral expectations from the guidelines, with flexibility in assigning consequences based upon individual needs.
- One DRC member presents the standards and guidelines while other members circulate around the groups, arranged by grade level. While finalizing expected behaviors, groups may work privately to finalize this section. By separating, groups will not overhear ideas that could limit the best growth. Groups are then brought back together to share.
- The DRC collects the team plans, reviews them, and returns to the teams with suggestions.

Tool # 5: A Sample Model for Grade-Level Standards, Guidelines, and Expected Behaviors

Queen City Middle School (or High School) standard for all grades: At Queen City School, I am responsible for all of my actions.

SIXTH GRADE THROUGH TWELFTH GRADE

Guideline 1: I will come to school prepared and ready to learn.

Expected Behaviors

Eighth grade students will:

- Attend school daily and arrive on time.
- Make up all work missed if absent from school.
- Keep desks, cubby spaces, and personal materials neat, clean, and organized.
- Take care of classroom items and school property.
- Bring textbooks to class each day.
- Bring appropriate learning materials as indicated by the teacher's supply list (i.e., paper, pencils, textbooks, markers, ruler).
- Cooperate with other students in class.
- Practice good-listening skills.
- Demonstrate self-control.
- Maintain high time on task.
- Follow the classroom daily routine.
- Talk only at appropriate times.
- Complete all assignments.
- Walk appropriately (no running).

Guideline 2: I will follow my classroom teacher's directions.

Expected Behaviors

Tenth grade students will:

- Follow the class's established routines.
- Answer and respond when acknowledged by the teacher.
- Do what is asked the first time directions are given.

- Actively participate in *all* class discussion and activities.
- Complete and turn in work as directed.
- Complete work in pairs or teams, or work independently as directed by the teacher.
- Practice responsible and civil behavior at all times.

Guideline 3: I will follow the directions from any adult in the school.

Expected Behaviors

Twelfth grade students will:

- Follow directions without question.
- Demonstrate civil behavior at *all* times.
- As seniors, be leaders.
- Follow all expected behaviors/procedures outside of the classroom.

Guideline 2: I will follow my classroom teacher's directions.

Expected Behaviors

Sixth grade students will:

- Follow the teacher's established class routine.
- Follow the teacher's procedures for movement in the classroom (i.e., turning work in, getting tissues, sharpening pencils).
- Listen attentively.
- Answer and respond when acknowledged by the teacher.
- Do what is asked the first time directions are given.
- Actively participate in class discussion and activities.
- Complete and turn in work as directed.
- Demonstrate responsibility.
- Be aware of words and actions, and use common sense and courtesy when speaking or acting.

Guideline 3: I will follow the directions from any adult in the school.

Expected Behaviors

Seventh grade students will:

- Listen attentively.
- Follow an adult request, promptly and politely.

- Respect and treat other adults (i.e., assistants, substitutes, volunteers, custodians, special area teachers) like their own teacher.
- Be attentive and cooperative.
- Practice responsible behavior at all times.
- Follow all expected behaviors/procedures for special areas and outside of the classroom.

Tool #6: Developing the School Consequences

- The faculty and staff must read Chapter 4 in detail prior to the session.
- The principal can use the narrated PowerPoint to direct the faculty and staff in developing or modifying any additional school consequences or school guidelines.
- Any faculty member can visit the section on consequences on the Web site.

**Tool #7: Sample Middle or
High School Model for School Consequences**

USING LOGICAL CONSEQUENCES

The responsible student develops self-discipline, which will build self-correcting mechanisms. Dedicated teachers work with all students as they strive to develop strategies to avoid instructional disruptions. However, when inappropriate behavior does occur, the student endures age-appropriate, logical consequences related to the behavior. RCM provides the opportunity for students to engage in self-reflection.

Guideline 1: I will come to school prepared and ready to learn.

A seventh grader comes to school with incomplete math homework. A logical consequence is for the student to complete the assignment during recess, lunch, or any other noninstructional time.

Guideline 2: I will follow my classroom teacher's directions.

A tenth grade science teacher asks a student to put away the items used during an experiment. The student returns to his seat, refusing to follow the directions to help classmates organize put away the materials. Restricting the student's movement to other activities during the period is a logical consequence.

Guideline 3: I will follow the directions from any adult in the school.

During class transitioning, a tenth grade teacher reminds a ninth grader of hall expectations. The student responds inappropriately and continues to demonstrate unsuitable behavior. A logical consequence for these actions is for the student to be taken to ICU.

SCHOOL STANDARDS, GUIDELINES, EXPECTED BEHAVIORS, AND CONSEQUENCES

School Standard

I am responsible for my actions.

School Guidelines

Guideline 1   Any serious or continuous student behavior that disrupts the educational process will not be tolerated.

Consequence   Observing adult takes the student to ICU and the ICU supervisor informs the homeroom teacher.

Guideline 2   Profanity or obscene language is not allowed.

Consequence   Observing adult takes the student to ICU and the ICU supervisor informs the homeroom teacher.

Guideline 3   Failure to respond to a reasonable request by an adult, or lying or cheating to deceive school authorities will not be tolerated.

Consequence   Observing adult takes the student to ICU and the ICU supervisor informs the homeroom teacher.

Guideline 4   Illegal or antisocial behaviors will not be tolerated. These classify as follows:

- Physically attacking or threatening to strike any school employee or any adult at school.
- Assaulting, attacking, or threatening to cause physical injury to a student by two or more students, and/or any assault resulting in serious personal injury by one or more students.
- Extorting or maliciously threatening another student to gain money or objects belonging to others.
- Possession of weapons.

- Arson, vandalism, unlawful entry, or theft.
- Selling, possessing, distributing, or being under the influence of alcohol, tobacco products, or other illegal drugs.
- Verbal threats, physical assaults, or intentional acts that clearly threaten the safety of others.
- Any act of a sexual nature.
- Directing obscene language and/or gestures toward any persons.
- Leaving class without teacher/principal permission.
- Breaking federal, state, or local laws.
- Violations of any school district behavior guideline.

Consequence   Observing adult immediate notifies principal to determine legal or other appropriate action.

Guideline 5   Students must not commit any other violations explicitly listed in the school guidelines or district middle or high school guidelines, or that the principal considers legitimate violations.

Consequence   The observing adult takes the student to the principal.

MIDDLE SCHOOL SCENARIOS

Scenario One

Christy and Lynn carry on a whispered conversation during a social studies lecture. It is not the first time.

Inappropriate Response

"Christy, Lynn, pay attention, please. . . . Girls, I'll tell you one more time. Stop talking. . . . Girls, every time you sit together you talk. Stop talking now and pay attention." The talking continues. It is ignored.

Acceptable Response

The teacher waits at the door for Christy and Lynn enter the classroom. A quiet conversation follows. "Girls, it has become obvious that when you sit together, you visit, regardless of what you should be doing. I think that it's great that you enjoy each other's company so much. However, it's not okay for you to carry on your conversations during class. I am assigning you seats on opposite sides of the room. When we are not actively involved in instruction and your work has been completed in a satisfactory manner, you may visit."

"Mrs. Hunt, that's not fair!"

"When you are not actively involved in instruction and your work has been completed in a satisfactory manner, you may visit. Christy, sit here, please. Lynn, over here."

RCM Response

As students work on an independent assignment, Mrs. Hunt calls the two girls to the door. She positions herself at the door to speak privately to the girls as she surveys the working students. "Girls, it's important that you have the opportunity to learn as much as you can in this class. When you sit near each other, you do not give adequate attention to your work. You talk too much. Your new seating assignments, effective tomorrow, are. . . . When your attention to instruction improves, I will give you an opportunity to return to your original seats."

Scenario Two

As students return to the classroom from the media center, Mr. Cline hears a scuffle behind him: "Mr. Cline, Mr. Cline, Marcus hit me on the head with his library book."

Inappropriate Response

Mr. Cline stops the line in the hallway and walks back to Marcus, finger pointing. "Marcus James, how many times have I told you to keep your hands to yourself? Don't you get tired of hearing me fuss at you? When are you going to start doing what you're supposed to do? Give me that book. When we get back to the classroom, start writing one hundred times, 'I must keep my hands, feet, and objects to myself.' You will finish it for science homework."

Acceptable Response

"Marcus, walk with me, please." Upon return to the classroom, Mr. Cline instructs the class to put away their library books and get out last night's math homework to review with a partner.

(Early in the year, Mr. Cline established a procedure for peer-homework check to precede group review.) He then speaks individually to Marcus. "Marcus this is the third time this week—and it's Wednesday—that I've had reports of your difficulty in maintaining self-control as we move through the building. For the remainder of the week your place in line will be next to me. Next week, you may return to the group. However, at the first report of you bothering others, your place will again be next to me. You are responsible for controlling your behavior in line." Soft grumbling and mumbling follow this directive. It is ignored. Marcus "forgets" to walk next to Mr. Cline for the next trip out of the classroom. Mr. Cline matter-of-factly directs Marcus to walk next to him. Marcus takes his time getting there. Mr. Cline calmly waits. It is necessary for Mr. Cline to repeat this exercise with Marcus at least three times before Marcus realizes that Mr. Cline means what he says. However, Mr. Cline's patience and consistency do result in an improvement in Marcus attitude and behavior.

RCM Response

Mr. Cline has observed, on previous occasions, that when students tell on Marcus for bothering them, Marcus does not show malicious intent with these interactions. He appears to want to establish a friendship, but just doesn't have the social skills to approach other students appropriately. Mr. Cline discusses with Marcus how someone with whom he would like to be friends might notice him in a way that does not appear threatening to that student. He also asks the school counselor to involve his class in guidance activities to assist Marcus and other students with similar needs, with approaching other students differently. These activities also help other students in the class recognize the difference between positive and negative attention from their peers more effectively.

Scenario Three

Sean calls out answers to many questions during the discussion of the story the class just read. This is not an isolated incident. Sean is a bright student, and his responses are on target. However, his interjections discourage many other students from volunteering to share responses.

Inappropriate Response

Ms. Staley acknowledges Sean's responses, sometimes asking additional questions to encourage further detail. She then reminds him to raise his hand and wait to be identified before he responds to future questions. The scene repeats.

Acceptable Response

Ms. Staley conferences privately with Sean and informs him that his continual callouts are unacceptable. Although she wants him to be part of the discussion, she informs him that after his first callout he will be removed to time-out and not allowed to participate in the discussion.

RCM Response #1

As Sean begins to call out his response, Ms. Staley looks at him, states his name, and raises her hand to remind Sean of what he is expected to do if he has something to contribute. She then calls upon another student to answer. Ms. Staley repeats this action each time that Sean calls out. She sometimes notifies Sean in advance that a question is for him. Sean eventually recognizes that his responses will not be acknowledged under his terms and begins to raise his hand. Although Ms. Staley does not call upon him every time he does so, she does tacitly affirm his compliance with procedures and privately recognizes his efforts to refrain from calling out.

RCM Response #2

Ms. Staley established a routine early in the year that provides wait-time before identifying someone to answer her questions. This holds all students accountable for forming mental responses. Students have role-played this in game situations. Ms Staley identified Sean's impulsiveness then. She recognized that this procedure did not stop Sean's callouts. She also noted other impulsive behaviors. Therefore, she brought her concerns about Sean's behavior to the attention of his parents and learning-assistance team. Appropriate individualized strategies were then created and implemented after discussion and observation indicated that Sean had attention deficit hyperactivity disorder.

HIGH SCHOOL SCENARIOS

Scenario One

As the students take an English test, pencil tapping starts near the back of the room. Students look up from their work to identify the source of the noise. It's Tony.

Inappropriate Response

Mrs. Walker walks back to Tony's desk. "Tony, get back to work. . . . Tony, that pencil tapping is distracting to the other students. Stop it. . . . Tony, if you don't stop tapping, I'll take away the pencil and you won't be able to finish the test. (This suits Tony.) Tony . . . "

Acceptable Response

Mrs. Walker walks back to Tony's desk and lightly but firmly places her hand on Tony's hand; the tapping stops. She removes her hand; the tapping resumes. Mrs. Walker quietly states, "Tony, stop tapping the pencil and complete the test now." The tapping continues. Mrs. Walker removes the pencil and test paper from Tony's desk. She tells him that arrangements will be made for him to complete the test after lunch.

RCM Response #1

Mrs. Walker learns from conversations with Tony's previous teacher and his parents that Tony unconsciously makes noises with objects in his hand as he concentrates on tasks. She observes other students as they test to see if Tony's actions disturb them as much as they disturb her. Other students appear unconcerned. Mrs. Walker ignores the tapping this time and plans to find a small sponge ball for the end of Tony's pencil so future tapping will not distract her.

RCM Response #2

It is obvious to Mrs. Walker that Tony taps his pencil to be disruptive. It affects other students' efforts to concentrate on the test. Mrs. Walker sends Tony to ICU and makes arrangements for him to complete the test after school. (Early in the school year,

Mrs. Walker communicated to parents how "afterschool detention" would be a consequence for some inappropriate behaviors. The majority of parents, including Tony's, supported her use of this strategy. As part of the arrangements, parents agreed to provide transportation home. In some instances, Mrs. Walker makes arrangements for a student to be in detention before school if this eases transportation problems for the parent.)

Scenario Two

Bobby gets out of his seat during a class discussion and begins roaming around the room.

Inappropriate Response

"Bobby, what are you doing?"
"I need a pencil."
"Bobby, you don't need a pencil right now. Return to your seat."
"But I need a pencil."
"Return to your seat now or I'll call the office."
"What did I do wrong?"

No matter what the teacher does now, Bobby has won and the teacher has lost. It will take several minutes to fully focus the rest of the class on instruction.

Acceptable Response

"Bobby, return to your seat."
"But I need a pencil."
"Bobby, return to your seat."
"But . . . "

Mr. Scott calmly arranges ICU for Bobby.

RCM Response

Mr. Scott has observed that Bobby has a tendency to get restless during class discussions. He is not an auditory learner. He easily distracts himself when he is not actively involved in instruction.

Therefore, Mr. Scott circulates during class discussions. He positions himself near Bobby's desk and occasionally refocuses Bobby's attention on the discussion by directing a question to him or lightly resting his hand on Bobby's shoulder. Mr. Scott has also found that Bobby is a doodler. His doodling does not appear to interfere with his ability to listen. It does help keep him in his seat.

Scenario Three

Blows are exchanged in the boys' restroom during lunch period.

Inappropriate Response

The staff member who broke up the fight takes the boys to the principal, who sends them home for the day (reward) *or* paddles both boys (punishes violence with violence).

Acceptable Response

The staff member who broke up the fight escorts the two students to their homeroom teacher(s). The teachers call the parents of both boys and arrange a conference. These students are directed to stay away from each other until a student mediation hearing can be scheduled.

RCM Response

The staff member who broke up the fight takes the two students to ICU. During investigation of the incident, the teacher learns that one student had been bullying the other, who finally had taken all he could take. The bully loses the privilege of moving through the school without adult supervision during lunch period. Arrangements are made with the school counselor for counseling. The teacher counsels the other student on acceptable responses to bullying by other students (specifically, avoiding situations in which such an outcome might result and informing a staff member when being victimized by a bully).

As the scenarios demonstrate, the teacher's words, the tone of voice, facial expression, and body movement can deliver expectations—subtlety and effectively—to students in a discrete, nonembarrassing manner. In each instance, what the teacher knows about the individual student influences the reaction to the behavior. Not all incidents of inappropriate student behavior can be resolved easily. However, teachers can limit the number of classroom disruptions through demonstrating how a student's unacceptable behavior, once identified, will be effectively addressed in a manner that is fair to that individual student. Sometimes disruptive behaviors cannot be satisfactorily addressed without causing increased disruption of instruction. A teacher's professional judgment and previous experience with individual students can then guide decisions about when ICU or behavior contracts are appropriate.

Tool #8: Developing Grade-Level Consequences

- The faculty and staff should read Chapter 4 in detail prior to the session.
- The principal can use the narrated PowerPoint to direct the faculty and staff in developing, sharing, and modifying a pool of grade-level consequences for not meeting expected behaviors.
- Visit the section on consequences on the Web site.

> **Tool #9: Sample Middle or High School Model for Grade-Level Consequences**

GRADE-LEVEL CONSEQUENCES

Expected Behavior

The student will not be in possession of cell phones, beepers, pagers, lighters, headphones, CDs, or other multimedia devices.

Suggested Consequences

- Adult confiscates items and parents may retrieve them.
- Item is returned at the end of the term.
- Item is not returned.

Expected Behavior

The student will dress appropriately. The student will follow the dress code.

Suggested Consequences

- Student receives verbal statement to go to restroom and reverse the clothes, if appropriate.
- Student changes into appropriate apparel.
- Teacher has conference with student.
- Student is sent home to change clothes.

Expected Behavior

The student will not wear hats or caps in the building.

Suggested Consequences

- Student receives verbal warning.
- Teacher or observing adult confiscates item and parents can retrieve it.
- With a second offense, the item is not returned.

Expected Behavior

The student will not have food or drink outside the cafeteria, with the exception of bottled water.

Suggested Consequences

- Student receives verbal reminder.
- Teacher or observing adult confiscates item and it is later returned.
- Student receives written disciplinary statement.
- Teacher has telephone conference with parent.
- Teacher or observing adult confiscates item and it is not returned.
- Teacher has parent conference at school.
- Teacher has counselor conference.

Expected Behavior

The student will be in possession of needed hearing aids, glasses, and other necessary devices.

Suggested Consequences

- Student receives verbal redirect.
- Teacher has counselor conference.
- Teacher or counselor develops contract with student and parent.

Expected Behavior

The student will attend all scheduled classes.

Suggested Consequences

- Teacher has telephone conference with parent.
- Student loses privileges for extracurricular activity.
- Student writes responsibility letter.
- Student receives afterschool detention.
- Teacher develops contract with student and parent.

- Teacher and/or parent assign chores/work detail.
- Parent shadows student at school.
- A teacher or assistant escorts student to and from class.
- Student attends Saturday school.
- Student misses practice for team sport.

Expected Behavior

The student will be prepared for class with completed homework.

Suggested Consequences

- Student receives verbal redirect.
- Student receives verbal warning.
- Teacher deducts five points on late assignment.
- Student receives a zero on homework.
- Teacher has conference with parent.
- Student loses special privileges.
- Student writes responsibility statement.
- Student completes homework during free time.
- Student completes homework during lunch.
- Student completes homework after school.
- Student receives afterschool detention.

Tool #10: Using the ICU, BIA I, and BIA II in the Middle or High School

RCM uses the ICU for behaviors schoolwide and within the classrooms that require further measure than consequences. The two most common reasons for ICU Placement are (1) major and continued disruptive behavior that literally stops the learning process for all students and (2) clear and intentional disrespectful behavior to an adult employee in the building. The DRC and the principal must approve ICU placement for any of other reasons. Keeping these reasons at the forefront can limit ICU abuse—the number one problem that can destroy an otherwise effective RCMPlan™. ICU should not be used for petty concerns, incomplete homework, or general talking. The ICU equates to what many consider grounds for school suspension.

In the case of disrespect, an accidental slip of a bad word without intent, and with the student quickly apologizing, may warrant a consequence for the use of inappropriate language, but not be grounds for ICU. A blatant act, such as a student cursing the teacher, referring to her with a vulgarity, is severe enough for ICU, as it fits the criteria for intentional disrespect. Usually, if the words are between two students, the behavior falls under a form of fighting and violates a board policy, which RCM does not address. Historically, teachers send students to ICU for disruptive behavior after every consequence has been tried. Also, while we do not encourage it, we have seen ICU used to correct tardiness and incomplete homework. Due to this variance, it is, again, up to the DRC, principal, and faculty to designate how ICU functions.

The most effective ICU that we have seen appears as we describe, but has covered windows blocking light. Ticking clocks hang at eye-level on each of four walls. This ICU so bores and frustrates student that they go out of their way to avoid return. This school has a 94 percent nonreturn rate. One time is enough.

ICU operates in a completely safe room with space for six to eight students, with chairs facing away from each other and no desks. Nothing hangs on the walls except a clock.

Once the principal and DRC finalize procedures for sending students to ICU, they determine support personnel. One person should supervise

ICU at all times with another adult changing every period or hour. Two adults must always be available for ICU supervision. One person remains and supervises while another goes to the classroom to pick up an ICU-mandated student—this is the best way for a student to arrive in ICU.

Once supervision is in place, the principal and DRC finalize the various procedures for ICU, including length of visits (usually 1 to 1½ minute per the student's age), sign-ins, counseling, return-to-class forms, and parent mailers. (More models and details appear in Chapter 4 and on the Web site.)

While determining these procedures, schools should remember that ICU's purpose—to allow time for reflection upon behavior then counseling—is 180-degrees different than in-school suspension (ISS). In fact, all of our schools have replaced ISS with ICU. ICU guidelines permit no schoolwork, and no talking or sleeping. Students who sleep usually are then required to stand, and students who talk are usually suspended. Since the ultimate goal is for the student to not return to ICU, ICU personnel must maintain a serious environment.

Chapter 4 provides details on when and how to use BIA I or II. BIAs are the most serious acts of misbehavior that do not break state laws or school board policies. Most BIA contracts are written for repeated serious offenses for disrespect and disruption. For a few students, ICU does not work. After the third visit to ICU, then, the student is bound to a BIA I; about half of the time, the behavior improves, discontinues, or reverses.

Students placed on a BIA II have very serious behavioral problems. Many times, schools can attain real help for these students, due to the detailed records available through RCM. For best results, we recommend viewing ways other schools have used ICU, BIA I, and BIA II on the RCM Web site.

**Tool #11: Sample Middle or
High School Model for ICU and BIA Procedures**

INTENSIVE CARE UNIT (ICU) PROCEDURES FROM TEACHER HANDBOOK

ICU Definition

The intensive care unit (ICU) is a supervised, isolated unit for students who do not respond appropriately to logical consequences prescribed in the classroom.

ICU Purpose

- ICU provides the teacher and student with time apart.
- ICU allows students to reflect upon their actions.
- ICU encourages students to refocus and receive guidance and direction from the teacher before returning to class.

ICU Location

- The small classroom is next to the office area in Room 444.
- The room contains only chairs and clocks.
- Chairs of varying sizes accommodate students of different ages and physical sizes.

ICU Hours

- Opens at start of school day (7:45 am).
- Closes at end of school day (2:45 pm).

ICU Staff and Duties

- Full-time coordinator: This individual oversees ICU monitoring. Jane Doe is the Queen City High School ICU Coordinator.
- ICU Assistant: Teachers, assistant principals (APs), and teacher assistants fill this position on a rotational basis; teachers serve one planning period for one week. (In some cases, teachers at most serve two weeks during the year.)

Schedules will be distributed to all school faculty and staff. Teacher assistants work in ICU for half of the school day, usually for two to three weeks over the entire year. Assistant principals usually serve as necessary or on call.

> Most teachers and APs enjoy the quiet time the ICU provides. Many elaborate on time for catching up on work, writing reports, etc. This is especially true when the ICU coordinator greets students or escorts students from the classroom to to ICU. Teachers can switch days of duty with each other if conflicts occur with absence, field trips, or major classroom activities. The ICU coordinator should be notified of any changes.

- Primary duties of ICU staff:

1. Escort students from classrooms to ICU (usually the coordinator).

2. Supervise students in ICU.

3. Record student responses to what happened in the classroom, hallway, etc.

4. Provide teacher coverage for classrooms when it is time for the teacher to pick up students.

- Communication: Both the coordinator and the individual on ICU duty carry walkie-talkies or cell phones for communication needs when one is outside of the ICU.

Reasons for Assigning a Student to ICU

A teacher may assign a student to ICU for two possible reasons:

- obvious disrespect to teacher(s)
- major disruption to classroom instruction

Procedures for Sending a Student to ICU

1. Call the direct line to the ICU classroom, extension 4444.

2. Provide only your name and classroom location to the ICU coordinator or teacher on duty. No other details are necessary. Do so quietly and without emotional display.

3. The ICU coordinator is dispatched to your location to pick up the student.

4. When the ICU coordinator arrives at your location, indicate the student(s) being sent to ICU.

5. The ICU coordinator removes the student and escorts the student to ICU. Do not send any materials or belongings with the student.

Initial ICU Procedure

1. The ICU coordinator signs in the student on the ICU register.

2. The ICU coordinator immediately assigns student to a chair.

3. The ICU coordinator directs student to sit quietly until a monitor can speak with the student.

4. A monitor sits down with the student and asks one question: "What happened in the last thirty minutes?"

5. If the student chooses to share, the monitor records the response on the ICU report. The monitor makes no comments and displays no judgment, either verbally or nonverbally. In most cases, the monitor is the ICU coordinator. The extra teacher in ICU adds extra supervision by being present in general and direct supervision when the ICU coordinator leaves to bring a student to and from the classroom.

6. The student is left to reflect upon the offending actions until the teacher who sent the student arrives and they meet in the hallway outside the ICU. When the discussion is finished, the student returns to class with the teacher. (If it is near the end of a period, the DRC should develop an alternate plan for best procedures.)

7. The DRC should develop a plan for blocked classes and ICU offenses broken with twenty minutes or less left in class. Some schools sign the student in to ICU and then allow the student to leave for the next class (if approved by the ICU coordinator). The student returns at the beginning of the period for the next class she has with the teacher who sent the student the day, or two days, before. All other procedures are followed. Most teachers feel that it is unfair for a student to miss part of a class if the offense did not occur in

that particular classroom. Schools should avoid this problem from the beginning.

Teacher Responsibilities
After Sending a Student to ICU

1. At your earliest convenience,* contact ICU to arrange for ICU assistance to cover your classroom.**

2. When the ICU teacher on duty or assistant arrives at your room, provide brief instructions for the classroom and then promptly report to the ICU.

3. Sit down with the student outside the ICU room.

4. Discuss and resolve the issue, *outside the ICU,* in a caring and firm manner.

5. Once convinced the student has resolved the problem and has the offending behavior under control, sign the student out of ICU and return to your classroom with the student.***

6. Complete the ICU report and return it to the ICU coordinator. The coordinator then makes and distributes copies to the appropriate individuals.

7. Determine the work the student will need to make up. This is a matter of teacher discretion. Provide the work to the student, as well as a reasonable deadline for completion.

Student Misbehavior in ICU

Unsolicited talking or disruptive behaviors constitute misbehavior. The principal immediately intervenes, and as determined by the principal, the student receives suspension.

---

*There is no designated time period a student should remain in ICU prior to your arrival to speak with the student. Use discretion based on the age of the student, the offense, student reaction, and student personality. No more than forty to forty-five minutes are recommended for middle and high school students. Most schools average twenty to twenty-five minutes.

**Schools using this approach may find two teachers assisting the ICU necessary. At no time should the students in ICU be left alone.

***If a student refuses to correct the behavior, you may call an administrator to intervene.

Behavior Improvement Agreements (BIAs)

Behavior Improvement Agreement I

- Students sent to ICU for a third visit are placed on a BIA I assigned by the DRC.
- The agreement approach in RCM makes a final attempt to improve behavior before major corrective action occurs.
- Students write descriptions of necessary improvement in their own words.
- The DRC determines and completes the consequences portion of the agreement. The consequences occur if the student breaks the contractual promises. In the BIA I, there may be just one consequence—a conference with an administrative team member. Another appropriate consequence for the teacher to mandate is a parent conference. (A school administrator must approve before initiating this consequence.)
- The student signs the agreement and the student, student's parents and teachers, and principal all receive a copy. The DRC keeps the original. A copy of the agreement is kept in a designated file in the school office.
- If no agreement is reached, the DRC notifies the principal.
- Upon notification of the third ICU referral, the DRC must complete a BIA I within five school days.

Behavior Improvement Agreement II

- Students who violate a BIA I contract are referred to the principal.
- The school administrator and the DRC use the BIA II as a final instrument prior to suspension.
- Regardless of when it is used, a BIA II includes promised behaviors, consequences, and the signatures of the involved parties.
- In designing an agreement, the principal may use the conditions from the BIA I and add stronger consequences.
- The principal may choose this approach for students who have not been successful in ICU or for those students who have delivered threats or acted abusively toward other students and faculty.
- The DRC determines and completes the consequences portion of the agreement. The consequences will occur if the

contractual promises are broken. However, the principal should designate two or three consequences, which might include therapeutic time-out from school, suspension, or legal action.

- The student and principal sign the agreement and the student, parents, and appropriate teachers receive copies. The principal keeps the original.
- If the student breaks the agreement, the principal takes the action necessary to administer the most appropriate consequence. With this approach, the student learns, for example, that suspension it is a result of the student's own action and not the principal's.
- Upon notification of a BIA I violation, the DRC has five school days to complete a BIA II.

Tool #12 Teaching Responsibility in an Inviting Environment

The DRC works with the faculty and staff, either in teams or with the faculty and staff at large, to develop an inviting environment for The RCMPlan™:

- Ensure everyone has read Chapter 2 in detail and arrives at training with a few ideas about designing the classroom and learning environment.
- Begin with selected examples from those offered at the end of Chapter 2.
- Ask teachers to share some ideas or plans they have developed to integrate learning responsibility within the major content areas.
- Use the Web site materials to further assist training during this session.

Tool #13: The RCMPlan™ Checklist

The DRC guides the faculty through a checklist relevant to The RCMPlan™ for their individual school, beginning with school guidelines through the BIA II, and concludes with a student guide and teacher handbook. Most checklists should include:

___school standard

___school guidelines with fixed consequences

___grade-level standard

___grade-level guidelines

___grade-level expected behaviors

___grade-level consequences and/or pool of consequences for violating expected behaviors

___narrative description of instructional plan for teaching responsibility in a warm and inviting environment (weekly or quarterly plans designed by teams or individual teachers)

___ICU design and appropriate use

___DRC procedures for ICU supervision and working with students and parents

___DRC procedures for BIA I and BIA II (including role of principal)

___design or modification of forms downloaded from the Web site

___activities for the first day of school (role of principal/ DRC/teachers)

___student packets or guides for inclusion with district policies/ state laws

___development of the teacher handbook

___RCM procedures for open house and/or parent visits (roles of principal/DRC/teachers)

Tool #14: Finalizing The RCMPlan™: Bringing It All Together

The principal rejoins the DRC for this final staff development. We suggest that for the first half of the period, the DRC assigns teachers to sit in mixed groups and not by grade and/or subject levels. During the second half of the session, teachers work in teams organized by grade level or subject area.

- The DRC distributes the entire RCMPlan™—complete for school and all grade or subject levels—including standards, guidelines, behaviors, logical consequences, ICU, BIA I and II designs and procedures, the teacher handbook, and the student guide.
- The faculty and staff complete an analysis on the alignment of the plan. For example, one group may find that a second grade standard is not related to the overall plan. There may be a perfectly good reason for the oddity, and this is the time it is questioned. Teams and faculty members work as an overall school team—as a family. If egos remain intact and defenses lower, a colleague may identify something that can be easily corrected instead of allowing a parent or a district office person to first make this discovery.
- Grade-level or subject-area teams develop more logical consequences. A school can never have enough consequences. Consequences from the lower grades can be shared with upper-level teachers and, often, a few minor adjustments can be made for another age group. Teams should spend time covering various scenarios and assigning appropriate consequences in a role-playing activity.
- Teams or individuals then share descriptions of three or four of the early lesson plans for teaching responsibility and civility, and how these plans integrate standard content and curriculum.
- Teams next discuss how students will be informed about the program. The best approach is usually for the principal to address each grade level in shifts, in the gym during the first day of school.
- Open house should be scheduled the night before the first day of school, or as soon as possible, for the principal and

DRC chair to provide an overview of the new plan and perhaps download the parent model for using RCM at home. The principal and DRC should be available for requested parent meetings for those having difficulty understanding The RCMPlan™.

- The principal and the DRC chair conclude the session with procedures for revising or updating materials, and provide details on how student guides and parent packets will be distributed during the first day of school.

Overall, faculty and staff should also walk away from the session understanding the following key components:

- The DRC and all educators in the school should watch for erratic patterns of a student returning to ICU the second time within a day or two. With proper planning, most schools do not see students in ICU until the second or third week. Some schools have such effective plans that ICU is used on an as-needed basis.
- When assigning any consequence at any level, faculty and staff involved with the situation should deliberate on whether this is the best action to take for the inappropriate behavior. Consequences should never be assigned when angry. Instead, a student can sit quietly until the situation can be handled calmly and professionally.

After the session, the principal and DRC devise a procedure for evaluating the effectiveness of The RCMPlan™ at all levels. A few days before school starts, it is often helpful for teachers to download the document from the Web site, "First Day, First Week, First Semester, and First Year." This document, focusing on how to give and gain respect to and from students, gives readers ideas for adding a few polished touches to their approach with each individual student. The RCMPlan™ will only be truly successful if students learn responsibility, civility, and respect.

References

Bushaw, W. J., & McNee, J. A. (2009). Americans speak out: Are Americans listening? The 41st Annual Phi Delta Kallap/Gallup Poll of the public's attitudes towards the public schools. *Phi Delta Kappan, 91*(1), 8–23.

Glasser, W. (1990). *Reality therapy.* New York: HarperCollins.

Horner, R. H., Sugai, G., Todd, A. W., & Lewis-Palmer, T. (2005). School-wide positive behavior support: An alternative approach to discipline in schools. In L. Bambara & L. Kern (Eds.), *Individualized supports for students with problem behaviors: Designing positive behavior plans* (pp. 359–390). New York: Guilford Press.

Purkey, W. (1989, June). *A review of the four invitations.* Keynote at the annual meeting of the Alliance for Invitational Education, Toronto, Canada.

Sugai, G. (2000). Instituting school-wide behavior supports. *CEC Today, 6*(7), 5.

Sugai, G., & Horner, R. H. (2002). The evolution of discipline practices: School-wide positive behavior supports. *Child and Family Behavior Therapy, 24,* 23–50.

Sugai, G., Sprague, J. R., Horner, R. H., & Walker, H. M. (2000). Preventing school violence: The use of office discipline referrals to assess and monitor school-wide discipline interventions. *Journal of Emotional and Behavioral Disorders, 8*(2), 94–101.

Index

CORWIN

A SAGE Company